TEACH YOU

D0671511

ISLAM

The *Teach Yourself World Faiths* series aims to present all the essential information required by the reader who has no previous knowledge of the religion, but who wants to feel confident in dealing with members of the faith community – both in terms of their beliefs and attitudes, and also the practical details of their culture, ceremonies, diet and moral views.

Titles to be included are:

Teach Yourself Sikhism
Teach Yourself Buddhism
Teach Yourself Hinduism
Teach Yourself Judaism
Teach Yourself Christianity
Teach Yourself Religion.

ISLAM

Ruqaiyyah Maqsood

TEACH YOURSELF BOOKS

Acknowledgements

The publishers would like to thank the following for their permission
to reproduce copyright photographs in this book:

Central Press Photos Ltd – p. 80; The Hulton-Deutsch Collection –
p. 78; Keystone Press Agency – pp. 18, 77, 81; Philip Emmett – p. 56.
All the remaining photographs were supplied by the author.

Every effort has been made to trace and acknowledge ownership of
copyright. The publishers will be glad to make suitable arrangements
with any copyright holders whom it has not been possible to contact.

Long-renowned as the authoritative source for self-guided learning – with more
than 30 million copies sold worldwide – the *Teach Yourself* series includes over 200
titles in the fields of languages, crafts, hobbies, sports, and other leisure activities.

British Library Cataloguing in Publication Data
  Maqsood, Ruqaiyyah Waris
  Islam. – (Teach Yourself Series)
  I. Title II. Series
  795.4

BP161.2
.M334
1994

Library of Congress Catalog Number: 94-6841-4

First published in UK 1994 by Hodder Headline Plc, 338 Euston Road, London
NW1 3BH

First published in US 1994 by NTC Publishing Group, 4255 West Touhy Avenue,
Lincolnwood (Chicago), Illinois 60646 – 1975 U.S.A.

The 'Teach Yourself' name and logo are registered trade marks of Hodder &
Stoughton Ltd in the UK.

Copyright © 1994 Ruqaiyyah Waris Maqsood

Typeset by Rowland Phototypesetting Ltd, Bury St Edmunds, Suffolk.
Printed in England by Cox & Wyman Ltd, Reading, Berkshire.

Impression number	14 13 12 11 10 9 8 7 6
Year	1999 1998 1997 1996

CONTENTS

Notes

As a mark of respect, Muslims may add 'Peace be upon him' when they refer to the Prophet Muhammad. In this book it is abbreviated as 'pbuh'.

Dates from the Muslim calendar are shown as AH (*Anno Hegira*), others are shown as CE (Common Era) which is equivalent to AD in the Christian calendar.

—— INTRODUCTION ——

——————— What is Islam? ———————

Islam is one of the three great faiths that sprang from the harsh land and deep silences of the Middle Eastern deserts. The other two are Judaism and Christianity and all three are interlinked because they are, in reality, worshipping the same One God. In historical terms, Islam is the youngest of the three, although Muslims argue that it is the earliest and forms the basis of all three.

Being a Muslim (a follower of Islam) has nothing, now, to do with being an Arab. The word 'Muslim' means simply 'one who submits'. The creed of Islam is a simple statement in two parts, *'La ilaha ilallah wa Muhammadur rasul al-Lah'* ('There is no God but Allah, and Muhammad is the Prophet of God'). Muslims accept these two basic things in the heart; that there really is One God, Supreme and Unique; and that the revelation given through the Arab prophet Muhammad is the genuine, final and complete revelation from this God, and supersedes all revelations that came before it.

Being a Muslim is essentially a very personal experience. It cannot be done 'second-hand'. It involves a moment (known as *ihsan* or realisation) of being 'born anew'. Every Muslim has to experience this if their Islam is to be a truly living thing.

Most people, once they become aware that God exists, rapidly develop *taqwa* or 'God-consciousness'. They become aware that everything they do, think or say, is done under the 'eyes of God'. It alters everything, from the simplest of deeds to the most momentous, because with *taqwa* there is a goal to be aimed at: to please God, Who can see them at every instant and knows every detail about them, even the secret unspoken thoughts of their hearts.

This God, by definition, is the Supreme, the Almighty One. It is not possible for there to be *two* Almighties, so there is only One God. This is the basic concept of Islam known as *tawhid* or 'one-ness', which is expressed in theological terms as monotheism (the belief that there can only be One God).

God, the Creator and Organiser of the universe, is so far above and beyond the limitation of the human mind that it would be impossible for anyone to grasp anything about Him at all, were it not for His desire that human beings should know and love Him, and try to live in a way that will bring them success and happiness. This is the second basic concept of Islam, known as *risalah* or 'prophecy'.

Muslims believe that there has never been a time since the creation of human thought when there were not revealers and people of insight. Many of these were the prophets named in the Bible. Most Muslims regard Adam as God's first messenger, and the builder of the first shrine dedicated to God's worship on earth.

The third basic concept of Islam is *akhira* or 'life after death'. Muslims believe that life on this earth is very far from being all that there is. Human life does not begin at birth, but at whatever stage God chose to create the living soul; it does not end at 'death', but at whatever stage God chooses to disintegrate that soul, if it is His will. The short period of time spent as a human being on this earth is for a reason: it provides a series of lessons and tests, the outcome of which is most important for each individual.

To pass the tests, which will sometimes involve much suffering, or perhaps being faced with the temptations of easy or corrupt living, a person needs a standard by which he or she can be guided. Each messenger or revealer of God did his or her best to teach this standard, but somewhere along the way followers with particular beliefs of their own, or with certain vested interests, coloured these teachings and diluted them. The message revealed to the Prophet Muhammad (pbuh) came in the form of words that had to be learned by heart and recorded with the utmost care and precision, and never altered in any way, so that there should be no doubt about them.

This revelation was given to the Prophet over a period of twenty-three years, and is now collected into book form, the book known as the *Holy Qur'an*. Muslims believe that the sacred words in the Arabic text of the Qur'an (obviously, it is a different matter for translations) are exactly as they were revealed to the Prophet, and have never been altered, edited, added to or taken away from, since he was given the messages in the 6th century CE. They are there for all time, a standard and a guide for the whole of life.

Although Islam began in the Middle East, and the revelation to the Prophet applied in the first instance to Arab people, it is a universal faith and has nothing to do with a person's nationality. Nowadays there are many millions of Muslims all over the earth, and Arab Muslims form only a small percentage of this vast *ummah* or 'family'.

There is only one form of superiority in Islam, and that is of genuine piety and humility, and desire to serve God. True service of God does not consist of rituals and recitations, which are only symbols of manifestations of religious awareness, but is a matter of the heart, the mind, and the soul. The most brilliant scientific discoverer with his flash of insight, and the most long-suffering ascetic saint with all his hours of pain and prayer, are not superior to the most simple goat-herd who is aware of God watching him while he watches his flock. They are of equal value to Him Who created all of them, set them in their individual paths, and Who loves them – despite their faults – with an intensity no human being can ever fully comprehend.

So that is the message and the 'ground-plan' of Islam. There *is* a God for real, and no God but the One, and the words and insights given to the Messenger Muhammad consist of true and genuine revelations from this Being, as relevant today as they were when they were first uttered some 1400 years ago.

> *'Righteousness is not a matter of turning your faces to East or West; but this is (true) righteousness – to believe in God and the Last Day, and the angels, and the Book, and the Messengers; to use your resources – out of love for Him – for your family, for those without family, for those in need, for the refugee, for those who ask (for your help), and for setting slaves free; to practise prayer and giving in charity on a regular basis; to keep all the promises you have made; to be steadfast and patient in pain and adversity, and throughout all periods of panic. Such are the people of truth, the God-fearing.' (Surah 2:177)*

1

THE LIFE OF THE — BLESSED PROPHET — MUHAMMAD (pbuh)

———— His birth and early life ————

The Prophet Muhammad (pbuh) was born in Makkah, Saudi Arabia, in around 570 CE, a member of the Hashim clan of the Quraish tribe. His father, Abdullah, a merchant, died before he was born, and his mother, Amina, died when he was only six years old, leaving him an orphan. He was reared first by his grandfather, Abd al-Muttalib, a man famous for his saintly life, and then by his merchant uncle, Abu Talib.

At this time, the people of Arabia were mainly superstitious pagans with a few notable monotheist exceptions, such as Abd al-Muttalib. Many Arabs lived nomadic lives on traditionally claimed territories, and there were only a few key cities such as Makkah, Yathrib and Taif. Makkah was a wealthy trading post that also happened to be the most important shrine for the Arab idols.

The cube-shaped Ka'aba temple claimed a very ancient history; it was said to have been built in the first place by Adam, the first created human being, and then rebuilt by Abraham the Prophet, and his son Ishmail. Originally, it had been a temple dedicated to the One True God, but over the centuries the Baal cults had predominated and at the time of the Prophet it was said to have contained no less than 360 statuettes and cult objects to minor deities.

The Prophet grew up a particularly devout and honourable man, a believer in One God, like his grandfather. He worked first as a shepherd, and then as a merchant, working for his uncle, Abu Talib. He became well known and well liked, and earned the nickname *'al-Amin'* ('the Trustworthy One') for his piety, honesty, fair dealing, and practical common-sense.

Later, he was employed by a wealthy widow, Khadijah, who, after a short while, offered herself in marriage to him, although she was in her forties and he was about twenty-five years old. Despite the age difference, they were very happily married and had six children. Even though polygamy was normal among Arabs at this time, the Prophet never considered any other marriage while she lived.

His call to be a prophet

His new position gave him security and much more time to devote to prayer and meditation. It was his habit to go off alone to the mountains around Makkah, and be close to God for long periods of time. Sometimes he would stay away for several days. He particularly used to favour the Cave of Hira on Jabal Nur (the 'Mount of Light') overlooking Makkah. On one of these occasions, in the year 610 CE, when he was around forty years old, something happened that changed his life entirely.

A presence he identified as the angel Gabriel was suddenly there with him, and he was shown words and ordered to recite them. He protested that he was not a learned man and could not read them, but the angel insisted, and suddenly the Prophet knew what the words said. He was ordered to learn them, and repeat them to others. Thus came the first revelation of verses of the Book now known as the Qur'an (the Recitation).

The night this happened was towards the end of the month of Ramadan, the month of fasting, and is known as *Lailat ul-Qadr*. It is celebrated on the 27th of the month, although the exact date is not known.

From this moment of calling, the Prophet's life was no longer his own, but in the hands of Him Who had called him to be a prophet, and spend the rest of his days in His service, repeating His messages.

After this vision, the Prophet had no further revelations for some time, and went through a period of trial and testing when he was not sure of the implications of what had happened to him. Then, after around two years, the messages began again, and continued for the rest of his life, a period of twenty-three years from the first revelation to the last.

His first converts were his wife, Khadijah, his nephew, Ali, a slave-boy, Zaid (both around ten years old and living in his household), and his friend, the merchant Abu Bakr.

The revelations

The Prophet did not always see the angel Gabriel when he had his revelations, and when he did, the angel did not always keep exactly the same form. Sometimes the angel was huge, filling the horizon, and sometimes the Prophet was only aware of eyes watching him. Occasionally, he just heard a voice speaking to him. Sometimes he revealed that the message did not come through clearly, but there was a sound like muffled bells, and this gave him a headache. At other times, the message was as clear and direct as if another person was just standing by him.

Sometimes he received the revelations when he was in deep prayer, but at other times they occurred 'spontaneously' while he was engaged in everyday life, out riding, or involved in conversation concerning the subject.

Every time he received a revelation, there was no doubt either in his mind or the minds of those observing him – he would suffer physical symptoms, like heavy sweating or a trance-like state, and he reported that he frequently felt as if he was going to 'have his soul snatched away'. Those who were with him could tell quite clearly when his revelations started and when they finished.

Many of those who rejected belief in what was happening to the Prophet accused him of being mad, or suffering from a disease, such as epilepsy; but there is no evidence whatsoever of that. A study of his life as revealed in the *hadith* (his own sayings, and reports of his teachings and way of life) show him to have been an immensely sane, kind, warm-hearted, down-to-earth person, and later an eminent and astute leader of his nation.

——————— His early mission ———————

At first, the Prophet did not preach in public, but spoke privately to those who were interested, or who had noticed the change in him. The particular way of Muslim prayer was revealed to him, and he began to practise this daily, which again drew comment from those who saw him. When he was given the instruction to begin preaching in public, he was ridiculed and abused as people scoffed at what he was saying and doing.

Also, many of the Quraish tribesmen – who had a vested interest in the Ka'aba shrine, since they provided the many pilgrims with food, water and lodging – were seriously alarmed as they realised his insistence on the One True God would undermine the prestige and credibility of the Temple worship, if people were converted to the Prophet's ways and began to abandon the worship of idols.

The way of life he taught became known as 'Islam', which means 'submission to the will of Allah', and his followers were known as Muslims, 'those who submit'.

Some of the Prophet's own uncles (such as Abu Lahab) became his chief opponents, vilifying and ridiculing him, and stirring up trouble for those who had been converted. There were many instances of torture and abuse, particularly against slaves and women who joined the 'new' religion. The first martyr of Islam was a woman, Sumayyah, and the first muezzin (caller to prayer) was the negro slave, Bilal, who was rescued from being left to die in the blazing sun with a huge rock on his chest.

Two large groups of early Muslims migrated to Abyssinia, where they took refuge with the Christian ruler, the Negus, who was so impressed with their teachings and way of life that he agreed to protect them.

The Quraish tribes decided to boycott the clan Hashim, and they were excluded from all trade, help, business and marriage arrangements, and were refused access to Makkah. It was a very difficult time, and many Muslims were reduced to absolute penury.

The Year of Sorrow

In the year 619, the Prophet's beloved wife, Khadijah, died. She had been his most ardent supporter and helper. In the same year his uncle Abu Talib, who had protected him from the worst persecution of the tribes, also died. The grief-stricken Prophet left Makkah and tried to make a fresh start in the town of Taif, but was rejected there also.

His friends arranged for him to marry a devout widow, Sawdah, who was a suitable person to look after him and had been one of the first Muslim converts. Aisha, the little daughter of his friend Abu Bakr, had known and loved the Prophet all her life. She was far too young for marriage at this time, but entered his household in a non-physical relationship that was considered quite normal in that culture.

The 'Night of Ascent'

It was during this year that the Prophet experienced the second most important night of his life, the *Lailat ul-Miraj* or 'Night of Ascent'. It is not clear whether this experience was vision, dream or psychic happening, but in it the Prophet was woken from where he lay sleeping, and taken by a miraculous beast to Jerusalem. From the site of the old Jewish Temple on Mount Zion, a way was opened for him through the heavens until he approached the Throne of God, in a region which even he and the angel Gabriel, who was accompanying him, were not allowed to enter.

During this night, the rules for Muslim prayer were revealed to him. They became the central part of the faith and have formed the keystone for Muslim life ever since.

He is also said to have seen and spoken to other prophets from the past, including Jesus, Moses and Abraham.

The experience brought great comfort and strength to the Prophet, and confirmed that Allah had not deserted him, or left him to suffer alone.

Dome of the Rock Mosque, Jerusalem.

— The Hijra – migration to Madinah —

The Prophet's fortunes now changed drastically. Although he was still persecuted and ridiculed in Makkah, his message had been heard by people outside the region. Some of the elders of the town of Yathrib invited him to leave Makkah and move to their town, where he would be honoured as their leader and judge. This town was the home of both Arab and Jewish people, and there had been constant conflict between them. They hoped Muhammad would bring them peace.

The Prophet immediately advised many of his Muslim followers to move to Yathrib, while he remained in Makkah as long as possible to allay suspicions. Without the restraining hand of Abu Talib, the Quraish were free to attack Muhammad, even to kill him, and this is what he realised they intended to do. They had no intention of letting him leave the city, or be received with honour anywhere else.

The Prophet's move was not without some drama. Ali, his nephew, bravely volunteered to stay in his bed as a decoy, and the Prophet evaded capture by using his knowledge of desert conditions. On a couple of occasions the Quraish were nearly successful in capturing him, but eventually the Prophet arrived at the outskirts of Yathrib.

So many people rushed out to offer him refuge in their homes that he was embarrassed by their kindness, and left the choice of place to his camel. The camel stopped by a place where dates were spread out to dry, and this was instantly donated to the Prophet to build his new home. The town took a new name – Madinat al-Nabi, the 'town of the Prophet' – which is now shortened to Madinah.

The people who had left Makkah were known as Muhajirun, the 'emigrants'. They were in the position of refugees, having left all their belongings in Makkah. The Prophet appealed to the people of Madinah to take them in and offer them homes. All those who volunteered to help the Makkan Muslims became known as Ansars, the 'helpers'.

———— The Prophet as ruler ————

The Prophet then set about creating a charter which would enable all the disputing tribes and factions in Madinah to accept him as head of state and abide by his decisions. He ruled that all the citizens should be free to practise their own religion in peaceful co-existence, without fear of persecution or ill-favour. He asked only that if there was any aggression or tyranny, they should join together and cooperate in the face of the enemy.

The previous tribal laws of both Arabs and Jews were replaced by the basic principle of general justice for all, irrespective of class, colour or creed. At first, the Jewish tribespeople of Madinah were in favour of the Prophet's rule; no Jew was ever forced to become a Muslim, and they were treated as equal citizens of Madinah. Later, trouble broke out when certain of the Jewish tribes did not keep the principle of supporting Madinah against attacks from outside, and they were regarded as renegades.

—— The Prophet's way of life ——

Every act and detail of the Prophet's life was of the greatest interest to those around him; his recorded deeds and sayings, the hadiths, ran into many thousands.

Although he was now ruler of a city-state, and in receipt of increasing wealth and influence, the Prophet never lived like a king. His home consisted of simple mud-brick houses that were built for his wives; he never actually had even a room of his own. Adjacent to these little houses was a courtyard with a well that became the mosque, the meeting place for the Muslim faithful.

It was taken for granted that the Prophet's life was 'public property'; the origin of the *hijab* or 'veil' grew out of the habit of the public claiming constant access to him and his hospitality, and the need to allow his family a little privacy. The original veil was a curtain separating their private quarters from the area where people came and went. The Prophet later taught that no one had the right to enter, or even to look into, other's houses without permission.

He believed strongly in good manners, always greeting people kindly, showing respect to elders, and balancing his serious teachings and reprimands with gentle good humour. He once said: 'The dearest of you to me are those who have good manners; the most offensive to me are the most boring and the long-winded!'.

He was never arrogant or superior, despite his position as leader; he never made people feel small, unwanted or embarrassed. He urged his followers to live kindly and humbly, releasing slaves as far as they were able, and generally showing practical charity, without thinking of reward. He said: 'Feed, for the love of Allah, the destitute, the orphan and the prisoner, saying: We feed you for the sake of Allah alone, desiring no reward from you, or thanks.'

His personal habits were extremely abstemious; he ate little, only simple food, and made it his practice never to fill his stomach. Sometimes he ate nothing but raw food for days. He slept on a very simple mattress on the floor, and allowed virtually nothing in the way of home comforts or decorations.

He did not regard it as right to sit down idly while others were working, and used to join in the housework with his wives, and helped in the various labour projects of his friends.

He owned very few clothes, and used to sew and patch his old clothes and shoes whenever the need arose. He regarded all material things as being no more than loans from Allah, to be used in His service, so whenever he was given anything, he usually gave it away to the needy.

All his recorded words and actions reveal him as a man of great gentleness, kindness, humility, good humour and excellent common sense, who had a great love for animals and for all people, especially his family.

——— The Prophet's life of prayer ———

The Prophet's life was spent virtually in a constant state of prayer, and in teaching his followers. Apart from the five compulsory prayers, which he led in the mosque, the Prophet also spent many hours in private prayer and contemplation, sometimes during the greater part of the night.

His wives prayed some of the extra night prayers with him, but after they had retired to sleep he was to be found standing or sitting in contemplation for many hours, snatching a little sleep towards the end of the night, before being woken for the pre-dawn prayer.

Like many in the hot climate of the Middle East, The Prophet made up for loss of sleep by taking a siesta during the heat of the day, after the midday prayer. Late afternoon was the time when the heat dropped again, and a major time of prayer, with the *asr* as the light began to change, and the *maghrib* after sunset.

One of his most famous prayers is known as the 'Prayer of Light':

> *'O Allah, place light in my heart, light in my sight, light in my hearing, light on my right hand and on my left, light above me, light below me, light behind me and light before me. O Allah, Who knows the innermost secrets of our hearts, lead me out of the darkness into the Light.'*

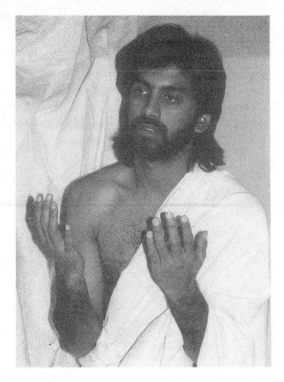

A pilgrim making
personal prayer.

——————— The Prophet's family ———————

The Prophet had a large family, his most intimate inner circle consisting
largely of women. He married twelve other wives after the death
of Khadijah, most of them mature widows who had suffered the loss
of their original loved ones. In three cases, the wives were daughters of eminent defeated enemies. Two of his wives were Jewish, one
was a Christian.

It is worth making the comment that people who do not understand
the reasons for Muslim polygamy frequently assume that the Prophet
must have been a 'sexual athlete'. At that time, the business of Muslims
taking several wives was rather like taking refugees into one's home,
but in a particularly kind and generous way; Muslim men were encouraged to look after the widows of their friends who died in battle, give

them separate homes of their own, and treat them equally in every respect (except, of course, in the matter of actual physical attraction).

The Prophet's wives were expected to share his devout way of life, and to make enormous personal sacrifice. They became known as the 'Mothers of the Faithful', and lived together as the centre of the Muslim religious community. It is on record that all of his wives were offered the free choice of whether they wished to live like this, or to leave him. They all chose to stay, even those with whom he had no sexual relationship at all.

The Prophet only had one further child, a son, who, like his two sons by Khadijah, died in infancy.

His four daughters all married and bore children. Of them, the most famous was his youngest daughter, Fatimah, who married his nephew Ali and gave him two grandsons, Hasan and Husain, and two granddaughters Zainab and Umm Kulthum.

Jihad

The Prophet was a man of peace and reconciliation, and would have preferred it if he had been left in peace in Madinah, but sadly, the opposition from the Quraish tribes continued and he was obliged to take part in warfare for the rest of his life.

His two most important early battles are known as the Battle of Badr and the Battle of Uhud. The Muslims won the first, but lost the second. As a result of this warfare, the many rules of conduct of war and treatment of prisoners were laid down for Muslims, the rules of *jihad*.

Jihad was never to be military activity for the sake of nationalism, tyranny or aggrandisement, but only for defensive reasons, and only until the enemy could be brought to peace. During the Prophet's battles, many of the enemy were converted to his side, impressed by the Muslim chivalry, courage and faith in God.

In March 627, his enemy, Abu Sufyan, raised a force of 10,000 men and advanced on Madinah, buoyed up by support from a Jewish tribe that had decided to oust the Prophet. After a two-week siege, the opposition withdrew, giving the Prophet a moral victory, for the eyes of Arabia had been upon him, and he had shown that even this vast army could not defeat him.

In the aftermath, the renegade Jewish tribe was dealt with severely. It is important to stress that on this occasion it was the Jews who were regarded as the incalcitrant fanatics, and not the Muslims. The Prophet always counselled mercy for defeated enemies, and never forced anyone to accept the faith of Islam against their will. On this occasion, however, it was a serious matter because the Jewish tribespeople were citizens of Madinah, and, therefore, under his leadership. They had signed the pledge of loyalty. The Prophet agreed to spare their lives so long as they repented their treachery and agreed to abide by the Muslim laws, but this they refused to do.

They were then allowed to appoint their own judge; but this judge had been so shocked by their treachery that said he would apply their own ancient law to them, and quoted Deuteronomy 7:2,

> *'When the Lord your God gives them over to you, and you defeat them, then you must utterly destroy them, and make no covenant with them and show no mercy to them.'*

All the men of the tribe were then put to the sword. It was intended to underline the point the Prophet was trying to make: that the laws of Islam had superseded those from the ancient past.

The incident had nothing to do with anti-Semitism, and shortly afterwards, as if to prove the point, the Prophet married one of the Jewish widows, Raihanah bint Zaid.

———— Pilgrimage to Makkah ————

In March 628 the Prophet dreamed of returning to Makkah, and decided to make this dream reality. He set out with some 1400 followers, all unarmed, in pilgrim dress of two simple white cloths. Although an increasing number of the citizens of Makkah had by now accepted Islam, the Prophet's followers were refused entry. Instead of making trouble, they offered their sacrifices outside Makkah, at a place called Hudaybiyah. The Quraish chief, Suhayl, came out and negotiated a treaty to keep the peace for ten years.

The Muslims repeated the pilgrimage in 629, and were allowed to visit the ancient tribal holy places undisturbed.

The surrender of Makkah and the —————— Final Pilgrimage ——————

The Prophet then began to plan for the peaceful surrender of Makkah. He also sent letters to the celebrities of the surrounding kingdoms, inviting them to consider Islam – the Roman Emperor, the Persian Emperor, the rulers of Egypt, Abyssinia and many leading chiefs – but only the Abyssinian accepted and was converted.

The truce of Hudaybiyah did not hold, and in November 629 the Makkans attacked one of the tribes that allied with the Muslims. The Prophet came down to Makkah with a force of 10,000 men, the largest army that had ever left Madinah. They camped outside the city, and Abu Sufyan (whose daughter had left him and become one of the Prophet's wives!) came over to his side. The Prophet promised a general amnesty if the Makkans would formally submit, declaring that all who took refuge with Abu Sufyan would be safe. In the event, only eleven people lost their lives.

The Prophet entered the city in triumph, went straight to the Ka'aba, and performed the ritual circumambulation seven times. He then entered the shrine and destroyed all the idols.

All the hereditary territories were left in the hands of their accustomed guardians, and the Prophet asked his followers who had originally abandoned property in Makkah when they moved to Madinah not to claim it back. Uthman ibn Talha, who had once refused Muhammad entry to the Ka'aba and persecuted him, was given back the key to the shrine, and it remains with his family to this day.

One by one the Quraish swore their fealty to the Prophet, and were pardoned.

Pilgrims gathered at the Ka'aba.

The Last Sermon

The Prophet did not live long to enjoy a peaceful rule. He returned to his home in Madinah, but his army was obliged to conduct further warfare against tribes that attacked them – tribes that had been shocked by the desecration of their idols at Makkah.

Events outside Arabia worked to the advantage of Islam. The western part of the Roman Empire was overrun by barbarians, and in the east the Byzantines at Constantinople had fallen into confusion through internal conflicts and inefficient rule. The Persian Sassanid Empire (which reached from Iraq to Afghanistan) had engaged the Romans in conflict for some thirty years, and had successfully attacked Jerusalem. By 630 the Romans had retaken Jerusalem, and the Persian influence was low, leaving a political vacuum for the warriors of Islam to occupy.

In March 632 the Prophet set out for his one and only true pilgrimage to the Ka'aba shrine, known as the Hajjat ul-Wida, the Final Pilgrimage. During this pilgrimage the revelations about the rules of the hajj were given to him, which are followed by all Muslims to this day. Up to this time pagans had been allowed to visit the Ka'aba as well as Muslims, but now all pagan influence was removed, and only Muslims were allowed into the city.

When the Prophet arrived at Mount Arafat for the 'Stand before Allah' (see page 80), he delivered what is known as his 'Final Sermon'. The summarised text of this famous teaching can be found in mosques all over the world:

'O people, listen carefully to what I say, for I do not know whether, after this year, I shall ever be amongst you again. Listen carefully, and report my words to those who cannot be here today.

Regard the life and property of every Muslim as a sacred trust . . . Hurt no one, so that no one may hurt you. Remember that you will indeed meet your Lord, and that He will reckon your deeds . . . You will neither inflict nor suffer injustice . . . Remember that you have rights with regard to your women, but they also have rights over you. Remember that you have taken them as your wives only under Allah's trust and with His permission . . . Treat them well and be kind to them, for they are your partners and committed helpers . . .

Worship Allah, say your five daily prayers; fast during the month of Ramadan, and give your wealth in zakah. Perform hajj, if you can afford to . . .

An Arab has no superiority over a non-Arab; a white has no superiority over a black, nor a black over a white, except by piety and good deeds. Every Muslim is a brother to every other Muslim . . .

No prophet or apostle will come after me, and no new faith will be born . . . I leave behind me two things, the Qur'an and the Sunnah; if you follow these, you will never go astray.'

At the end, he received his final revelation:

'Today I have perfected your religion for you, and I have completed My blessing upon you; and I have approved Islam as your religion.'
(Surah 5:5)

There was a silence, and then the voice of Bilal rose over the hushed enormous crowd, calling them to prayer.

The death of the Prophet

When he returned to Madinah, he began making preparations for an expedition to the Syrian border, but he was already ill with a heavy fever.

He continued to attend and lead the prayers in the mosque as far as he was able, supported by Ali, and eventually requested Abu Bakr to take his place.

He did not recover, and eventually collapsed. His wives realised that he wished to be with Aisha, and moved him to her room, where he died in her arms on 8th June, 632 (in the Muslim calendar this is 12 Rabi'ul Awwal, 11 AH).

He was sixty-three years old. His last words were said to have been: 'I have chosen the most exalted companions, in Paradise.'

His followers found it hard to believe their Prophet could have died like a mortal man, but Abu Bakr reminded them of the revelation after Uhud:

> *'Muhammad is but a messenger, and messengers have passed away before him. If he die, or is slain, will you then turn back?' (Surah 3:144)*

He was buried in Aisha's room, which is now a shrine and part of the modern mosque complex at Madinah.

2

—— THE SUCCESSION ——

—— The 'Rightly-Guided Caliphs' ——

After the death of the Prophet the new *Caliph* (Successor) was to be someone who had been with him in both Makkah and Madinah, qualified to pass on correct hadith, and whose life was so similar to the Prophet's that it exemplified the sunnah. Such a person would be able to make decisions as binding as those of Muhammad himself; the first four caliphs were regarded to fulfil these criteria, and are therefore known as the 'Rightly-Guided' Caliphs or *Rashidin*.

Although the caliphs increasingly had access to enormous wealth, they continued to live simple lives, as the Prophet had done, and were famous for their saintliness and humility.

Abu Bakr (632–634)

Although the Prophet had given several indications that his cousin and son-in-law Ali should have been the next leader, he requested Abu Bakr to lead the prayer when he was too ill, and there was strong feeling that the leadership should go to one of the 'elders'. Abu Bakr, in his sixties, had been the Prophet's first adult male convert and was the father of his dearly loved wife Aisha. He was respected for his gentleness, wisdom, piety and humility. As Caliph, he was known as As-Siddiq (the Witness to the Truth) and Amirul Muminim (ruler of the believers).

His short reign consisted largely of warfare, mainly against those Arab tribes that decided to turn against Islam (known as the Ridda Wars).

On his deathbed, Abu Bakr did not give the community the chance to elect the next caliph, but nominated Umar. Ali considered this to be wrong, but accepted the decision.

Umar (634–644)

Umar's caliphate was also spent in warfare. Jerusalem fell in 638, the Christian ruler Sophronius declaring that he would surrender to none other than Umar himself. Umar behaved with great consideration to the Christians by refraining from offering prayer in the Shrine of the Holy Sepulchre, so that it was not turned into a mosque.

Although the Muslim army conquered territory successfully, no individual was forced to be converted to Islam at the point of the sword, as is often suggested. The Qur'an specified quite clearly: 'Let there be no compulsion in religion. Truth stands out clear from error.' (Surah 2:256.) The formula was 'Islam, tribute, or the sword', the sword being reserved for those who refused to cooperate and pay the appropriate taxes. Those who did convert to Islam lived tax-free.

In 644 Umar was assassinated by a Firoz, a Persian Christian slave, who had been brought to Madinah to embellish the simple mud dwellings that had been the home of the Prophet. He was stabbed six times at the dawn prayer, and died three days later.

Uthman (644–656)

As Umar lay dying, he elected a group of six people to choose the next leader, one of whom was Ali, but Uthman (who had been the husband of two of the Prophet's daughters) was chosen. In his reign the Muslim empire spread west across North Africa and east to the boundary of China and the Indus Valley.

Although Uthman was a saintly man, he was also a wealthy member of the Ummayyad clan of the Quraish, and in his rush to provide governors for the newly acquired territories, he foolishly promoted too many of his own relatives, and was accused of nepotism. His cousin Mu'awiya, for example, was created Governor of Syria.

The Muslims of Kufah and Fustat protested, and tried to persuade the eighty-year-old Uthman to abdicate. Uthman preached a fiery sermon against them, in the face of all good advice. Soon afterwards, while he was at prayer, a group of these Egyptians killed him. His wife Nailah tried to protect him, but her fingers were cut off. She sent them, with her plea for help, to his cousin Mu'awiya in Syria.

Ali (656–661)

At last, twenty-four years after the Prophet's death, Ali (also known as Asadullah – the Lion of God) claimed to be the rightful successor, but Aisha still opposed him, supported by the Prophet's old friends Talha and Zubayr. She accused him of being lax in applying justice, because he did not seek out the killer of Uthman. Aisha led her army against him, but was defeated in the Battle of the Camel in 656. She was captured, but treated with respect and returned safely to her friends in Madinah, where she lived until she died.

Next, he was opposed by Mu'awiya, who had by now been Governor of Damascus for twenty years, who also refused to recognise him until the assassins of Uthman had been brought to justice. The implication was that Ali had supported them, since he had not tried to track them down and punish them. Their armies met at the Battle of Siffin, but the crafty Mu'awiya made his troops put leaves of the Qur'an on the end of their spears, so Ali's pious soldiers refused to strike them down. Ali agreed to accept arbitration, in which both sides should stand down and face new elections, but this was tantamount to accepting that he was not the rightful caliph. His most pious warriors were shocked that Ali should have agreed to this and seceded from his ranks, becoming known as the Kharijites (Seceders).

Ali was given many premonitions of his fate, including even the name of the man destined to kill him. Despite this he refused to hide or run away. He was struck down by a Kharijite while praying in the mosque at Kufa, and during the three days it took him to die, he protected and fed his assassin, ordering that he should be spared if he lived, and killed with one stroke if he died.

Mu'awiya

Mu'awiya seized the chance to have himself elected caliph. Ali's son Hasan agreed to waive his rights and accept a pension; Ali's second son, Hussain, agreed to leave his claim until the death of Mu'awiya.

Mu'awiya decided not to move to Madinah, and Damascus became the capital of the Muslim world. On his deathbed he nominated his son Yazid as successor instead of Hussain.

The Kharijites never accepted Yazid, however, and formed the Shi'at Ali (Party of Ali and his descendants). The Shi'ite revolt peaked with the Battle of Karbala, in which Hussain was slaughtered.

From Mu'awiya onwards, the Caliphate became hereditary. The first dynasty is known as the *Ummayyad.*

(For those interested in further study of Muslim history and Muslim sectarianism, see the recommended book list.)

Shi'ite Islam

Shi'ites claim that Sunni Islam is not the true Islam at all, but the creation of the lax and worldly Ummayyad caliphs backed up by the eminent but rather pedantic Muslim jurists of the 9th and 10th centuries CE, and that Shi'ite Islam is actually older and more closely based on the political practices of the Prophet and the original four Caliphs. Sunnis reject this point of view, and claim that they represent authentic Islam – which is practical, tolerant and compassionate – and the Shi'ites, in their quest for personal purity and interest in the theology of that which lies beyond human understanding, represent an intolerant, speculative and extremist form of Islam.

Shi'ites are frequently regarded as troublemakers in the West because they will not accept a status quo that goes against their principles; their zealots preach revolution and martyrdom, and have been behind numerous uprisings and civil wars. Their enemies generally regard them as fanatics and terrorists, who interpret the verses about jihad in the Qur'an to mean that they should put all their energy into conversion of the world by driving away the devil and all his works. (The West is typically known as 'the Great Satan'.)

Shi'ite Muslims claim that the Prophet had always intended Ali to be his successor after his death, and had declared it at the gathering of Ghadir Khum, but while Ali was involved in burying him, the Prophet's close friend Abu Bakr (father of the Prophet's wife Aisha, between whom and Ali was some bad feeling) took control. (Sunnis interpret the speech at Ghadir Khum as being no more than an acknowledgement of Ali's merit, and not a nomination for succession.)

Ever since the caliphate passed to Mu'awiya and other Ummayyads after him, who were not direct descendants of the Prophet, the Shi'ites have agitated to replace them with a true descendant on the throne of a united Islamic Empire.

They reject the Sunni principle of 'the consensus of the community' (*ijma*) and substitute the doctrine of the Imam or spiritual head directly descended from Ali. They believe that the choice of Imams is divinely determined by birth, not left to human error, and that part of their inheritance is their divine and superhuman knowledge, which is infallible.

Other key Shi'ite differences from Sunni Islam are their belief that God has foreknowledge of all human action, but does not predestine it; a different form of call to prayer and ritual ablution before prayer; the permission of temporary marriage (*muta*) which was repealed by the Prophet after initially allowing it; the (sometimes excessive and rather superstitious) veneration of shrines and tombs of Imams, and the permission to conceal their beliefs (*taqiyya*) in order to avoid persecution and suffering, or argument with Sunni colleagues.

3

THE QUR'AN

The compilation of the Qur'an

The Qur'an was revealed to the Prophet bit by bit over a period of twenty-three years. Muslims believe that it is the Word of Allah, exactly as the Prophet received it, and in this sense it is different from any other of the world's holy books, since they were all created by human authors many years after the deaths of the prophets involved, and were then edited and revised and added to by disciples. The Qur'an contains nothing but the revelations from Allah, not one word of it being the creation of the Prophet. He was nothing more than the transmitter. (The Prophet's own teachings and sayings run into many thousands and are known as *hadiths*.)

As each revelation was given, the verses were learnt by heart and jotted down on whatever materials came to hand – dried-out palm leaves, pieces of broken pottery, ribs and shoulder bones of sheep, bits of leather and white stones.

A single verse is known as an *ayah* (plural *ayats*, meaning 'signs'), and a chapter is a *surah*. There are 114 surahs of varying lengths (all except the ninth beginning with the words 'In the Name of Allah, the Most Compassionate, the Most Merciful'), and 6,616 ayats – a total of 78,000 words in Arabic.

The surahs are not in chronological order, however. It is generally accepted that the first words are in surah 96:1–5 and the final words are in surah 5. The order was also something revealed to the Prophet, who had to recite the whole collection revealed so far to the angel

Gabriel every Ramadan, and the entire text was checked with the angel twice, shortly before the Prophet died.

The first surah is called *al-Fatihah* (the Opening). Each surah is named after some striking incident or word in it, so some have strange names like *al-Baqarah* (the Cow) and *al-Ankabut* (the Spider). Others have names of Allah, for example, *al-Nur* (the Light), *al-Nazir* (the Warner), *al-Majid* (the Glorious). The Cow is actually about religious duties, divorce laws and rules governing fair conduct of war.

Islam began at a time when books were the property of only the rich, and people had the habit of learning a great deal by heart. Anyone who knew the full text of the Qur'an was known as a *hafiz* (plural *huffaz*). However, when many of the original huffaz were slain in battle, people began to worry how the accuracy of the text would be checked after the Prophet's death. They were beginning to repeat the verses and jot them down in their own dialects, and this brought with it a danger of personal interpretation, misinterpretation, and alternative versions.

The first Caliph, Abu Bakr, requested the Prophet's companion, Zaid ibn Thabit, to make a complete written version in one Book. He did not alter the messages in any way; no explanations or editorial comments were added. This text was given to the Prophet's widow Hafsah, the daughter of Caliph Umar. In the reign of Caliph Uthman, some twenty years after the Prophet's death, any other written versions which individuals had were either checked for full agreement against this one, or destroyed. Numerous copies of the 'standard' text were made and sent to all chief Muslim centres, and all copies since then have been identical.

The earliest known Qur'ans that still exist are in Tashkent and Istanbul. Modern technology has now taken over the task of the copyist; the Tashkent Qur'an has recently been photocopied.

The art of Calligraphy

Calligraphy means 'beautiful writing'. The early scribes concentrated on finding styles worthy of the words they were putting down.

The master writers believed that a person's handwriting revealed their inner character and nature, so only a spiritually pure person should attempt the task.

The first hand-written Qur'ans had no artwork, because the scribes believed it was wrong to make representations of heavenly (or even human) beings; and they did not wish people to pay attention to the decoration rather than the content of the verses.

Later, the wealthy sultans commissioned lavish and colourful Qur'ans resplendent in gold, green, red and blue.

The most famous scripts used in Arabic calligraphy are known as Kufic (from the Islamic centre at Kufah) and Nashki. Eighth century Kufic has formal, simple lines easily drawn on parchment or inscribed on stone, but so angular and ornamented that only a practised eye can read it. The more cursive Nashki style is easier to understand, and was more easily done with pen on paper. It more closely resembles today's printed style.

How respect is shown to
——————— the Qur'an ———————

If Muslims have the space, the Qur'an may be kept in a special room which is kept clean and used only for prayer and reading the holy Text. Others make a shelf high up on the wall, so that nothing can be placed higher than it. When not in use, the Book is usually wrapped in a cloth, so that no dust may fall on it.

Text used as a wall-decoration is also respected, and usually placed on a wall people face, so that no back is turned to it.

When the Qur'an is in the room, Muslims are expected to behave with reverence, so it would not be proper to act indecently, rudely, cruelly or selfishly. One should not have the television on, watching a violent film, for example. The Qur'an imparts an atmosphere of prayer – it is the silent reminder of the Muslim submission to Allah.

While the Qur'an is recited aloud, Muslims should not speak, eat or drink, smoke, or make any distracting noise.

Before touching the Qur'an, Muslims should be in a state of *wudu* (see page 52.f), or at least wash their hands. Muslim women would usually cover their heads as for prayer, and a woman who is menstruating or has recently given birth should not touch it.

Muslims start their studies at an early age.

Before beginning to read, the Muslim prepares the heart by consciously thinking about Allah and seeking refuge from Satan (Surah 16:98). They adopt a special position, so that the body is disciplined and alert, often sitting on the floor with the Qur'an on a special stand (called a *rehl* or *kursi*) in front of them. It is disrespectful to place the Qur'an on the floor.

Reading with heart, soul, mind and strength is known as *tilawah,* and the practice of correct pronunciation (usually learned in the mosque school or medrassah) is called *tajwid.* Some Muslims do not speak Arabic, and learn how to recite the verses without understanding what they mean. However, as they progress in Islam they should also learn the meanings, and see how the messages apply to them and how they should alter their own lives.

When the reading is finished, the Qur'an is put away carefully. It is never left on a table, where someone might put something down on top of it!

Translations of the Qur'an into other languages are not regarded as being quite the same thing as the Qur'an itself, and most Muslims in countries where printed books are commonplace are used to the idea of translations being handled and treated casually in shops, libraries, classrooms, and so on. It is perhaps important to realise, however, that a Muslim might be shocked rather than flattered by a non-Muslim student, not in wudu, pulling a Qur'an out of his pocket to have a quick read in the pub!

Studying the Qur'an.

4

THE KEY TEACHINGS
- OF ISLAM REVEALED -
IN THE QUR'AN

—————— Tawhid and Shirk ——————

There are three basic concepts in a Muslim's awareness of God – His One-ness, His Transcendence, and His Immanence.

God's Unity or One-ness is known as *tawhid*, 'There is no God but Allah'. Muslims reason that if God is the First Cause, Creator and Supreme Force in the universe, there can only be One by definition, because it is impossible to have two 'supremes' or 'first causes'.

Nothing is remotely like God, and nothing can be compared to Him. Nothing shares His power, and He certainly does not have partners, or any kind of 'family'.

> *'He is Allah, the One. Allah is Eternal and Absolute. None is born of Him. He is Unborn. There is none like unto Him.' (Surah 112)*

God is only referred to as 'He' because it is traditional, He has no gender; this is why Muslims prefer to use the word 'Allah' rather than 'God', which has a female form, goddess. All the names of God revealed in the Qur'an reflect qualities and not sexuality, for example, *al-Badi* (He Who creates out of nothing); *al-Batin* (He Who knows the latent and hidden properties of things); *al-Muqit* (the Controller).

Many times He is called Rabb, or Lord; but never once in the entire twenty-three years of revelations did He call Himself Abb, or Father. This cannot have been accidental. The word 'Father' has human and sexual connotations, and although Muslims are aware of God in an intimate and personal way, they think of Him as Creator rather than Father. To a Muslim, the concept of 'father' has dangerous implications that can lead into *shirk* (the division of the unity of God).

God knows and sees everything; He is totally 'other' from His created universe, outside time, eternal, without beginning or end.

> *'No vision can grasp Him, but His grasp is over all vision. He is above all comprehension, yet is acquainted with all things.' (Surah 6:103)*

It is impossible for humans to imagine what He is like, except as He chooses to reveal it. Our concepts are always limited, but He revealed that He is absolute Order, Justice, Mercy, Truth and Love, and many other concepts.

He is the Owner of everything; what humans think they own is allotted to them by God's will, should be used in order to do His will, and should be given back to God in due course.

The Love and Compassion
of Allah

This is His most important aspect. God is not only Creator, He is also Judge, and the eternal fate of every living being lies in His 'hands'. Thankfully, the justice of Allah is not the same as that of human beings, who have incomplete knowledge, or who can be vengeful. God knows every thought and motive, every influence acting upon a person.

His mercy is far greater than any humans have the right to expect, or that they show to each other.

> *'If God punished us according to what we deserve, He would leave on earth not one living thing.' (Surah 34:45; 16:61)*

> *'O My servants, who have transgressed against their own souls! Do not despair of the mercy of God, for Allah forgives all sins. He is the Compassionate, the Merciful.' (Surah 39:53)*

Many humans, of course, find this hard to accept, either because they are too proud, or too hard-hearted, or too despairing, or for many other reasons. Nevertheless, the mercy of Allah is repeated constantly throughout the Qur'an and is a main subject of the hadith.

> *'O son of Adam – so long as you call upon Me and ask of Me I shall forgive you for what you have done . . . Were you to come to Me with sins as great as the earth itself, and were you then to face Me, ascribing no partner to Me, I would forgive you in equal measure.'*
> *(Hadith Tirmidhi, Ahmad)*

Similarly, Muslims are expected to forgive those who sin against them, to treat them with gentleness and 'cover' their faults (Surah 3:159).

Angels, the Devil and jinn

The universe consists of that which is seen and understood by our five senses, and that which is unseen (known as *al-Ghaib*).

What we see and understand is only like the tip of the iceberg in the vastness of God's creation.

The two most important non-physical created entities of which some humans are aware, and in which Muslims believe, are *angels* and *jinn*. They may take any shape or form in order to be seen by humans when they wish it.

Angels are the agents and servants of God, the means by which He governs the universe and the channels by which humans become aware of Him. They are sometimes seen by people in times of crisis; many sensitive people feel aware of their presence when they pray and meditate.

Each human is assigned two special angels as guardians and 'recorders'; they note down every good and evil deed in each person's 'book', the record on which they will be judged on the Day. If a person repents, the record of the evil deed is wiped out.

> *'Surely those who say "our Lord is Allah" and who follow the straight path, the angels descend upon them saying: "Fear not and do not be sad . . . we are your protecting friends in this life and in the next."'*
> *(Surah 41:30–31).*

A few angels are named and have specific roles: Gabriel (Jibreel) brings messages to the chosen ones, and is frequently referred to as the 'holy spirit' in the Qur'an; Michael (Mika'il), is the protector of holy places and life-sustainer in times of trouble; Azra'il takes away the souls of the dying; Israfil is the angel who calls the souls on Judgement Day; Munkar and Nadir are the questioners; Malik, the keeper of Hell; Ridwan, the keeper of Paradise. Jinn are also non-physical beings, and they can be either good or evil, having free-will like humans. They are thought to inhabit unclean places, and can often frighten and confuse human beings by involving themselves in their lives and homes. Occasionally they attempt to possess human bodies and have to be exorcised. They are not always malevolent, however, and surah 72 mentions jinn that were converted to Islam.

The Devil, Shaitan or Iblis, is the chief of the jinn. He refused God's command to honour the newly created humans because he thought he knew better than God. Out of jealousy, he became the enemy of all humans, determined to lead people's hearts and minds away from God. (See Surah 15:28–31; see also 2:36; 3:36; 4:117–120; 5:94; 7:200–1, 8:48; 15:17,34; 16:98–100; 22:52–3; 24:21; 35:6; 36:60.)

Human beings

Human beings are the highest physical creations of Allah, and possess both material and spiritual characteristics. Each being has a distinct individual soul (the *rouh*). It is the soul and not the body the soul lives in, that is the real person.

Human beings are all descended from an original couple created by God; Adam and Eve. Muslims regard the theory of evolution as no more than a theory, for which there is little evidence; apes were created in their own image, and still exist as apes, and so on.

Humans have an allotted time-span, over which they have no control. They were intended to be God's deputies (*khalifas*) on earth, responsible for the care of the planet.

They are created equal, but do not remain equal because they exercise free-will; they can love and be kind, or hate and be destructive. Their worth is not measured in intelligence or status, but in submission to God and right living.

─────────── **Tests** ───────────

Life is not seen as random with no point, but as a test for the life to come. We are allotted circumstances, talents, and so forth, and are tested in the use we make of them.

> *'We shall certainly test you with fear and hunger and with the loss of goods or lives or the fruits of your toil. But give encouragement to those who patiently persevere, and, when calamity befalls them, say: "We belong to Allah, and to Him do we return." (Surah 2:155–156)*

Some are tested with poverty or ill health – will they become despairing, dishonest, or show patience and faith? Others are tested by being rich – what use will they make of their riches? Will they become selfish, greedy, or act with responsibility? It is pointless to bewail one's lot – all situations can be reversed in a second if God wills; the Muslim's duty is to accept, remain firm, patient and faithful, and seek to do God's will in whatever circumstances they find themselves.

────── **Risalah – Revelation** ──────

If the Muslim's duty is to serve God and do His will, it is God's duty to explain clearly what that will is, otherwise the individual cannot be held at fault. *Risalah* is the channel of communication from Allah.

Before the Blessed Muhammad there was a whole chain of prophets (tradition says 124,000), including the twenty-six named in the Qur'an. These include celebrities known from the Bible; Noah (Nuh), Abraham (Ibrahim), Moses (Musa), John the Baptist (Yunus ibn Zakriyah), Jesus ('Isa), and many others (peace be upon all of them). Three are not named in the Bible; Hud, Salih and Shu'aib (though this last is believed to be the same as Jethro, Moses' father-in-law).

Prophets who merely taught and did not write are called *nabi*, and those who left books are called *rasul*. Of the holy books, four are mentioned in the Qur'an; the *Tawrat* (or Torah) revealed to Moses, the *Zabur* (or Psalms) of David, the *Injil* (or Gospel) revealed to Jesus, and the *Sahifa*, scrolls dictated to Abraham. The last book is completely lost, and Muslims believe that the others are not to be identified with the contents of today's Bible which are compilations and editions written many years after the times of the prophets concerned.

All the prophets are messengers from the One God, and are to be respected and believed, and Muhammad (pbuh) is regarded as the 'seal' of the prophets, the last messenger.

Jesus

Jesus (pbuh) is regarded by Muslims as one of the greatest of all prophets, the miracle worker. It is always made very clear in the Qur'an that he was not to be thought of as Divine, a Son of God, in the Christian sense. Muslims believe in his virgin birth, but that this was a miracle of God in creating a child without a father, not that it made the miraculous child in any way a part of God.

Throughout the Qur'an there are verses reminding Muslims that to believe that God has partners or a family is *shirk* and a fundamental misunderstanding of the nature of God.

The Qur'an indicates that Jesus was not overcome by death, and this is generally taken to mean that God rescued him from crucifixion, and that he ascended alive into Heaven (Surah 4:157). His function was not as a sacrifice to save people from their sins – for every person will be judged as an individual, and no one will bear the sins of another – but to be a messenger of God and to show the way to Him.

Akhirah – Life after Death

Muslims believe that the human soul lives only once on earth, and after death faces a Day of Judgement, and an eventual fate in either Paradise or Hell (*Jannam* and *Jahannam*).

After death, the body is buried and the soul of the good person may expand without limit, while the bad person is cramped in the grave. On the Day, God will resurrect all people, and recreate their decomposed bodies, down to the details of their fingerprints (Surah 45:24; 75:1–4).

Heaven and Hell are frequently described in graphic physical terms; Heaven, or Paradise, being like a beautiful garden, where people become young again and enjoy untainted pleasures, and Hell being a terrible, scorching place of torment, sorrow and remorse. However, although many Muslims take the descriptions literally, there are also clues in the Qur'an that they should be considered symbolically, since Heaven and Hell are not physical dimensions at all, and our future state lies beyond the scope of our limited human knowledge.

'In Heaven, I prepare for the righteous believers what no eye has ever seen, no ear has ever heard, and what the deepest mind could never imagine.' (Hadith Qudsi, and Surah 32:17)

'We will not be prevented from changing your forms and creating you again in forms you know not.' (Surah 56:60–61)

Islam teaches that God does not wish to send anyone to Hell, and they will only be obliged to go there if they insist on evil living without repentance, and treating the truth of God as a lie.

Some Muslims interpret Hell as being rather like a hospital, where the cure may be painful and drastic, but in the end the patient is made whole.

——— ál-Qadr – Pre-destination ———

Muslims believe that the entire universe is under God's control and direction, therefore nothing can take place without His ordaining it. There cannot be such a thing as a random or chance event. (See Surah 35:2; 57:22.)

Everything is known (even the number of hairs on your head), and everything that happens is an expression of His will, and has purpose and meaning. God alone is the source of benefit or harm, and to turn to anything else for protection or help is futile.

This idea of pre-destination is difficult to reconcile with the other Muslim concept of free-will, but Islam should not be considered a fatalistic religion. The whole point of sending messengers from God to give revelations is to allow humans to use their free-will; the whole point of human life is a test, which would be totally pointless if God had pre-destined human choices.

Fatalism renders people helpless and weakens their sense of responsibility, a criticism frequently made of Muslims who misunderstand the importance of revelation and free-will. No prophet ever taught fatalism.

Although everything in the universe is governed by natural law, human beings are not governed in the same way that the Sun and Moon are, for example. We are warned that we are under Law, and the breach of Law brings penalty. This applies on both the physical and moral levels; if we don't wish to be burned, we must keep our hands out of the fire. It makes no difference whether or not we knew in advance that fire would burn. If we don't wish to suffer heartbreak, we must keep ourselves from immoral and selfish living.

The Sun is the source of light, but if we choose to close the curtains, it will become dark for us. If we stay in the darkness too long, our eyesight will suffer. These misfortunes occur according to natural laws, the outcomes of which God knows in advance, but we choose how we will act, and are judged accordingly.

5

— WORSHIP — IBADAH —

Ibadah comes from the word 'abad', meaning a slave or servant. Ibadah is therefore service of Allah, or slavery to Him. Basically, it is what Muslims mean by 'worship'. However, for Muslims, worship is not something confined to special days or particular prayers, but it involves a conscious awareness of God throughout the day, every day, and a conscious desire to carry out His will in every sphere of activity.

Ihsan

Muslim worship really begins with the concept of *ihsan* or realisation. It is perfectly possible for a human being to go through all sorts of forms of worship, prayer and other ritual without really being truly aware of the presence of God. Human nature being what it is, this rather barren worship can happen to anybody from time to time. However, ihsan implies that a person really is making a conscious effort to be 'in communication' with God.

There is a very famous hadith recorded by Caliph Umar, one of the Prophet's best friends, that describes ihsan. The Prophet was one day approached by a traveller in very white clothing, who sat down with him knee to knee, and asked the Prophet to tell him about Islam. This traveller was the angel Gabriel, the very one who had revealed the messages of the Qur'an to the Prophet. One of the direct questions he asked was for a definition of ihsan. The Prophet replied that it meant one should worship God as though one could see Him, for He sees you even though you do not see Him.

Awareness of God (also known as *taqwa* or God-consciousness) leads to deepened consciousness of the importance and meaningfulness of

'In Communication with God' – this Muslim girl wears a prayer veil.

the gift of human life, and the desire to make the very best of it while one has the chance.

Iman

The word *iman* means 'faith'. When the same traveller (Gabriel) asked the Prophet to define iman, he replied that it was to believe in God, His angels, His books, His prophets, and the Last Day, and the decreeing of both good and evil. We have already considered the implications of iman in the previous sections.

Amal

Amal means 'action'. Muslims see no point in academic beliefs or doctrines unless they are translated into action. The whole point of Islam is to submit to Allah and direct one's life into carrying out His will to the utmost of one's ability.

The concept of amal can actually be divided into two categories. The first is to obey the command of Allah in the practice of the five disciplines known as the 'five pillars', which will be described shortly. The second is to do one's best in every aspect of daily life and routine to follow the *sunnah* or practice of the Prophet, or at least the principles behind the sunnah (if one is dealing with some aspect of modern society that was beyond the personal experience of the Prophet) so that every single thing one does is for the greater glory of God. That way, the Muslim believes he or she will keep on the right path, and will find peace, satisfaction, justice and happiness.

Jihad

Jihad is often thought to mean military activity, but this is not the true meaning of the word. Jihad means 'striving'; obviously it can have a military context (see page 85ff), but the true jihad is the battle against what Muslims call *dunya* (literally, 'the world'). The world, as creation of God, is not in itself an evil thing or place, but there are certain aspects of material existence which are directly opposed to the will of God.

Amr bin Auf recorded:

> *'It is not poverty which I fear for you, but that you might begin to desire the world as others before you desired it, and it might destroy you as it destroyed them.' (Hadith Bukhari and Muslim)*

The most basic wrong thing is love of self. Once again, the self is a creation of Allah, and something to be loved, cherished, cared for and respected. But when a person becomes *selfish* then they are putting their own base greeds and desires before right living, and love of self has become a form of shirk. People who are selfish are worshipping themselves rather than God; they are certainly putting themselves before their duties towards God, which are generally expressed in our love and concern towards others, whether people or animals.

Thus, dunya represents the lure of the world's luxuries and lusts that lead people away from the right way and influence them to become miserly, greedy, cruel, cowardly, arrogant, callous and so on. Jihad is the fight against this tendency.

'The life of the world is but a past-time and a game. Lo! Real life is the Home of the Hereafter, if you but knew it.' (Surah 29:64)

Hakim ibm Hizam recorded:

'Riches are sweet, and a source of blessing to those who acquire them by the way; but those who seek them out of greed are like people who eat but are never full.' (Hadith Bukhari)

Abu Huraira recorded:

'Richness does not lie in an abundance of worldly goods, but true richness is the richness of the soul.' (Hadith Muslim)

Taking all these concepts together, ihsan, iman, amal and jihad make up the Muslim concept of ibadah; worship of Allah. This is why Islam is not just a matter of ritual, prayers or fasting or feasts; it is the conscious bringing of every moment of the day, every decision, every detail of one's thoughts and actions, into deliberate line with what one accepts as being the will of Allah.

6

THE PILLARS
OF ISLAM

—— Shahadah – bearing witness ——

The first 'pillar' of Islam is *Shahadah* or bearing witness to the faith.
It is a simple statement of creed that falls into two parts: that there is no
God but Allah, and that Muhammad (pbuh) is His genuine messenger. It
comes from the word 'ash-shadu' which means 'I declare' or 'I bear
witness'.

In Arabic, the words are:

'Ash-shadu an la ilaha illallahu wa Muhammadur rasulullah.'

When people make this declaration and truly believe it in their hearts,
then they have entered the faith (see Introduction, page 1). There is
no ceremony like a Christian baptism; what counts is the conscious
awareness and firm conviction that one genuinely does hold these two
beliefs.

Sometimes a new Muslim will talk things over with an *Imam* (teacher),
or have a course of study sessions; once the new Muslim takes the
decision to become Muslim (or realises that he or she is Muslim), their
first act is to declare the faith publicly, in front of two witnesses. From
that moment of public witness, they are Muslim.

However, it is not just a matter of reciting words; it is something that
has to be believed with all one's heart, because following this declaration

the Muslim is intended to trust God with all his or her heart, and hand over their life to His service.

Making this decision can cause some pretty drastic changes. Being a good witness involves far more than words; your whole life must back up what has been declared. Most people coming into Islam in the Western world have to change a great deal of their diet and lifestyle; they have to give up pork products, any animal products that are not *halal* (permitted), alcohol, entertainment based on the social giving of alcohol, immodest dress, and so forth. They also have to give up arrogance, selfishness, deceitfulness, and many other weaknesses of character.

The Shahadah is also used for the call to prayer five times per day. If the mosque has a tower, a man known as the *muezzin* or *muadhdhin* climbs up and calls aloud:

Allahu Akbar! (four times)
Ash-hadu an la ilaha illallah (twice)
Ash-hadu ana Muhammadur rasulullah (twice)
Hayya alas salah (twice)
Hayya alal falah (twice)
Allahu Akbar (twice)
La ilaha illallah. (once)

In English, these words mean:

'God is the Most Great!
I bear witness that there is no God but Allah.
I bear witness that Muhammad is the Prophet of Allah.
Come to prayer!
Come to success (or salvation)!
God is the Most Great!
There is no God but Allah!

At the end of the first prayer of the day the phrase 'It is better to pray than to sleep!' is added – '*as-salatul khairum min an-naum*'.

This call to prayer is known as the *adhan*, and it gives Muslims time to get ready if they are going to attend at the mosque. Just before the actual start of the prayers, a second call to prayer is uttered before the congregation, known as the *iqamah*. It is the same as the adhan, except that the words '*qad qamatis salah*' – 'The prayer has begun' – are added before the final Allahu Akbars.

Other times that the shahadah is pronounced are at the birth of a new baby, first thing on waking and last thing before going to sleep at night, and if possible, they are the last words in the hearing of a dying person.

Salah – prayer

The philosophy of prayer

'O you who believe! Be steadfast in prayer and regular in charity, and whatever good you send forth for your souls before you, you shall find it with God; for truly God sees all that you do.' (Surah 2:110)

Ibn Mas'ud recorded:

'I asked the Messenger of Allah (pbuh): "Which of all deeds is the most pleasing to God?" He replied: "To offer the obligatory prayers at their due times."' (Hadith Muslim)

Prayer is the second pillar of Islam. Prayer in general terms means being conscious of God and communicating with Him in some way or another, and Muslims try to maintain an attitude of prayer and be constantly aware of God throughout the day. However, the prayer ritual of *salah* is somewhat different from the casual making of appeals to God of a personal nature. It is perhaps better translated in English as 'worship' rather than 'prayer'.

Salah is a particular ritual of movements and words (each sequence of which is called a *rakah*), some of the words repeated as part of the regular routine, and others chosen from the Qur'an by the Muslim as he or she wishes. This prayer is one of the five things laid down as *fard*, or 'compulsory', for a Muslim. Allah requires those who submit to carry out this prayer five times per day, at certain set times. Although these times are not laid out in detail in the Qur'an, the five can be deduced by putting two passages together. The hadith of the Prophet gives more precise details. The Qur'an states:

'Give glory to God when you reach eventide and when you rise in the morning; yes, to Him be praise in the heavens and on earth; and in the late afternoon and when the day begins to decline.' (Surah 30:17–18)

'Celebrate the praises of your Lord before the rising of the sun, and before its setting; yes, celebrate them in the watches of the night,

and at the sides of the day, that you may have spiritual joy.' (Surah 20:130)

There is usually a reason for everything in Islam, and the reason why salah has to be said five times is because that was the number revealed to the Prophet on *Lailat ul-Miraj*, the Night of Ascent. The Prophet felt that fifty times would be a good idea, but the Prophet Moses reasoned with him that this was far too demanding for the ordinary worshipper, and eventually the number was set at five.

The five daily prayers are now known as *Fajr* (the morning prayer between dawn and sunrise), *Zuhr* (just after the height of the midday sun), *Asr* (during the afternoon when the shadows have lengthened), *Maghrib* (just after sunset), and *Isha* (during the hours of darkness).

The prayer times deliberately avoid the exact times delineated by sunrise, midday and sunset because of their pagan connotations of sun worship. At those exact times, Muslims are actually ordered *not* to pray.

However, the times are obviously related to the sun's progress through the day, and since times of sunrise and sunset change according to the seasons and the country in which one lives, these days Muslims usually have timetables showing the exact moments when the prayer times begin and end. (In the United Kingdom sunrise comes very early in summer months; Muslims are allowed to go back to bed after they have performed their fajr prayer!)

Since many Muslims go to the mosque to pray together, they also have timetables for congregational prayer, for obvious practical reasons. Many mosques set up little clock faces showing these times, five for the daily prayers and one for the special Friday prayer.

Muslims regard it as preferable that men meet together in congregation to pray, but women are generally encouraged to pray in the home. However, there is nothing to prevent women coming to congregation if they so wish, and it is not compulsory for men to attend every single prayer in the mosque if they prefer to pray elsewhere.

Salat al-jama'ah

Only one congregational prayer in the mosque is regarded as compulsory, the midday prayer on Fridays – *salat al-jama'ah* – also known as *salat al-jumah*. The word 'jama'ah' means 'congregation' or 'gathering', and the word 'jumah' simply means Friday. All adult male Muslims are expected to attend, and are thought to have left Islam if they don't attend for more than three weeks. In Islamic countries all shops and businesses close during this time, so that men can go.

> '*O believers, when proclamation is made for prayer on the Day of Congregation, hasten to God's remembrance and leave business aside; that is better for you, did you but know.*' (Surah 62:9)

Even Muslim men who are negligent about the other daily prayers make an effort to gather at the mosque on Fridays. During the special service, the key features are the two *khutbahs* or sermons given by the Imam. The Congregational Prayer itself consists of only two *rakahs*. After this, people can pray individually, and then go back to work.

Having allowances made for Friday prayer is one of the difficulties confronting workers and students in non-Muslim countries.

It is sometimes possible to make up a congregation in the workplace or school, but Muslims always consider it preferable to meet together in the full congregation at the mosque, wherever possible.

Individual devotion, not priests

A non-Muslim observer might think that Muslim prayer is nothing but formalised ritual, and people wishing to be critical could no doubt discover examples of where this is indeed the case.

However, in the age-old conflict between 'priestly' religion and personalised and accountable faith, Islam comes down solidly behind the latter. Historically, organised religion always seems to have been a battle between those who claim that only special priestly figures, with special knowledge of how to perform the ritual and carry out sacrifices accurately, are effective, and those who claim that such formalism is meaningless before a God who requires personal morality and devotion. (Some people in the Christian faith would no doubt see the historical conflict between the 'Romanism' of Roman Catholics and the 'Protest' of Protestants in the same terms.)

For many simple folk in pre-Islamic times, worship had become little more than a vast system of sacrifice, the value of which depended not so much upon the moral conduct of the individual worshipper as on the qualification of the officiating priest. Priests monopolised the number, length and terminology of prayers, the liturgies and dogma, and were largely responsible (even if unintentionally) for the notion that an individual could turn up to a congregation once a week to make up for the spiritual and moral deficiencies of the other six days.

There are no priests in Islam. No monopoly of spiritual knowledge or special holiness intervenes between believer and God. No sacrifice or ceremonial is needed to bring the anxious heart nearer to the Comforter. Each Muslim is his or her own priest, no individual being denied the possibility of drawing near to God through his or her own faith. Islam recognises the dignity and responsibility of every individual human soul; each person faces God on a one-to-one basis, in worship which is a most heart-felt outpouring of devotion and humility before God.

The practice of the Prophet has, however, attached certain rites and ceremonies to Muslim prayer, and this is the most obvious aspect of it to an observer; it should be pointed out in unmistakable terms that it is to the devotional state of the mind that the Searcher of the spirit looks. Prayer without the presence of the heart is to no avail; devotion without understanding is a useless empty formalism and brings no blessing. Mere external or physical purity does not imply true devotion, but rather a sense of pride and religious hypocrisy. It is purity of heart and mind, and humility of spirit that bring an individual close to God.

Imams

The person who stands before the congregation leading the prayer is not in any sense a priest, but simply a person who has volunteered to lead, someone who is respected, had some knowledge of Muslim faith, and who knew enough of the Qur'an to recite during the prayer. Most mosques have a regular Imam these days, but this is not a compulsory requirement, and any Muslim may lead the prayer in his absence, or when the prayer is being carried out elsewhere, for example, in the home.

If men and women are praying together, the leader is always the man; it could even be a very young man – there are hadith showing how a seven-year-old boy led prayers during the Prophet's lifetime. If women are praying together, one of the women leads from the middle of the row. A male Imam stands just in front of the other worshippers, who form lines behind. If there are only two worshippers, the Imam stands on the left with the other worshipper on the right hand side, just a few inches back.

The purpose of prayer

Muslim prayer is intended to purify the heart and bring about spiritual and moral growth. The aims are to bring people close to Allah; to bring a sense of peace and tranquillity; to encourage equality, unity and brotherhood; to develop gratitude and humility; to demonstrate obedience; to train in cleanliness, purity and punctuality; to develop discipline and will-power; to draw the mind away from personal worries, calm down passions, and master the baser instincts.

Preparation for prayer

Niyyah

The first part of prayer is *niyyah* or intention. By closing the mind to all worldly distractions (whether pleasant or unpleasant ones), the worshipper begins to make ready for prayer. Although prayer can be said at any time in any place, the Muslim prepares for salah by making his or her own body physically clean, and by selecting a clean place in which to pray, if possible. If one prays in the desert or by the roadside, one is not able to dictate conditions, but in Muslim countries there are usually little areas marked out and set aside for prayer and kept in a clean condition. In the home, or at the mosque, prayer is usually said on a carpet. It may be an individual prayer-mat, or – at the mosque – the floor is usually carpeted or covered with rush-matting, with lines marked out on it so that the worshippers may arrange themselves in orderly fashion.

Prayer-mats are usually small colourful rugs, decorated with abstract designs or depicting some holy mosque. They frequently show the Ka'aba and the mosque at Madinah where the Prophet is buried. The only significant point about the design is that it should not depict living beings. Otherwise, any mat will do.

Clothing

Muslims should wear clean clothes for prayer, as far as possible. They remove their shoes, but it is not necessary to remove socks, stockings or tights. Men must be covered at least from waist to knee, and women must completely cover themselves, leaving only face, hands and feet visible, and should not wear perfume (which might distract the men).

It is preferred if women do not wear make-up or nail polish, although staining the nails with henna is acceptable.

It is not compulsory for men to cover their heads, but many wear a special prayer-cap, often of white lace.

Young Muslims at prayer in a school-room. Notice the prayer-caps and prayer-mats.

Wudu

There is a difference between everyday washing away of dirt and becoming purified for prayer. Purification (*taharah*) is a mental as well as a physical cleansing. Before prayer, Muslims perform the ritual wash

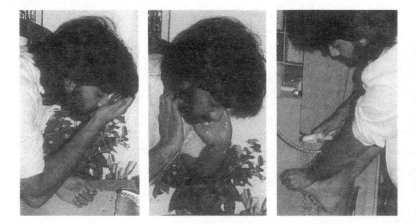

Wudu – the ritual washing.

known as *wudu* or *wuzu*. Cleansing certain parts of the body in running water.

> '*O you who believe! When you rise up for prayer, wash your faces and your hands as far as the elbows, and wipe your heads and wash your feet to the ankles; and if you are under the obligation to perform a bath then go through the complete wash; and if you are sick, or on a journey, or have come from the privy or have been intimate with a woman, and you cannot find water, then take clean earth and wipe your faces and your hands with it. Allah does not wish to put you into difficulties, but He wishes to purify you that He may complete His favour on you.*' (Surah 5:6)

The Prophet taught:

> '*Wash your hands up to the wrists three times; rinse your mouth three times with water thrown into your mouth with the right hand; sniff the water into the nostrils and blow it out three times; wash the entire face, including the forehead, three times; wipe the top of the head once with the inner surface of both hands together; wash your ears with your forefingers and wipe the back of the ears with your thumbs, and wipe the back of your neck once; wash the right foot and then the left foot up to the ankles three times; let the water run from your hands up to your elbows three times.*'

The washing is always done in a quiet, prayerful manner, for it is in itself part of the act of worship. While washing, Muslims pray that they will be purified from the sins they have committed by hand or mouth, that they will be empowered to do good and refrain from evil, and that they should walk on the right path and not go astray.

If water is not available, the worshipper can perform a dry 'wash' known as *tayammum*, which simply involves touching clean earth and wiping over the face, hands and arms in an imitation wash.

Muslims are not required to make a fresh wudu before every prayer if they have remained 'in wudu' between times. Wudu is broken if a person has sexual intercourse, or if any discharge leaves the body (such as blood, seminal fluid, urine or faeces, or wind), or if the person has lost consciousness through sleep or other cause. Women who are menstruating, or are in the days after childbirth, cannot enter wudu and are excused from salah prayer at these times.

A full bath, known as *ghusl*, is necessary after sexual intercourse, when menstruation has finished, and after contact with dead bodies.

If socks are worn, it is not considered necessary to wash the feet every time; so long as they are in wudu at the first wash, Muslims may simply wipe over the socks with wet hands the next time, although many Muslims regard this as laziness.

Qiblah

All Muslims, when they pray, turn to the direction of Makkah. They usually know its position in advance, but if they are in a strange place they can ask, work it out from the position of the sun, or use a small compass.

There is a consolidating effect of fixing a central spot around which to gather the religious feelings of Muslims throughout the world. Muslims do not believe that God somehow lives at Makkah, or in the Ka'aba sanctuary, much less that they are worshipping the famous black stone set in one of its corners.

When the Prophet was first taught the salah, he used to turn in prayer towards the Jewish sanctuary at Jerusalem. This was significant for Arab converts to Islam, because it meant they specifically had to turn their backs on their old holy place, the Ka'aba. Later, when the Prophet was established in Madinah, he was ordered by Allah to turn towards the Ka'aba as the new *qiblah*, indicating that it would soon be cleansed of all its idols and restored to the worship of the one true God.

In the spiritual sense, the true qiblah means to turn the heart in the direction of God – and He, of course, cannot be located in any physical direction whatsoever.

The barrier

If they are praying in the open, Muslims usually mark off the area of their prayer with a barrier which separates them from any people or animals passing in front of them. The Prophet used to stick his staff into the ground, just to the right of him, in case there might be any thought that he was in some way bowing down to it as one might bow down to an idol.

The practice of prayer

The series of movements and accompanying words are known as *rakahs*. These always follow a set pattern.

During the rakah there are eight separate acts of devotion. The first, after niyyah (conscious intention), is *takbir*, the deliberate shutting out of the world and its distractions, delights and miseries. Muslims stand to attention, and raise their hands to the level of their shoulders, and acknowledge the majesty of God. They say 'Allahu Akbar' – 'God is the Most High'.

Second, they place their right hand over the left on the chest, and say 'Glory and praise be to You, O God; blessed is Your name and exalted is Your majesty. There is no God other than You. I come, seeking shelter from Satan, the rejected one.'

After this comes the recital of the first surah in the Qur'an, surah al-Fatiha (the Opening).

The words are:

> *'Bismillahir rahmanir rahim. Alhamdu lillahi rabbil alamin, arrahman irrahim, maliki yawmiddin. Iyyakana abudu wa iyyakana stai'in. Ihdina siratul mustaqim, siratul ladhina an'amta alaihim, ghairil maghdubi alaihim wa laddallin. Amin.'*

The translation is:

> *'All praise be to Allah, the Lord of the Universe, the Most Merciful, the Most Kind, Master of the Day of Judgement. You alone do we worship, and from You alone do we seek help. Show us the next step*

Muslims at prayer in a Mosque.

*along the straight path of those earning Your favour. Keep us from
the path of those earning Your anger, those who are going astray.'*

Next, another passage from the Qur'an is recited; the choice of the
prayer-leader. It can be long or short, but the Prophet recommended
keeping recital short for public prayers (where people in the congregation might be suffering discomfort, illness, coping with children, or
have business to attend to), and whatever length you liked for private
prayers.

A favourite short surah is al-Ikhlas (the One-ness):

*'He is God the One; He is the Eternal Absolute; none is born of Him
and neither is He born. There is none like unto Him.'*

Next comes *ruku*, the bowing. Men rest their hands on their knees
and bow right over with a straight back; women do not bow quite so
deeply. This bow is to show that they respect as well as love God.
They repeat three times:

'Glory be to my Great Lord, and praise be to Him.'

The next state is *qiyam*, when they stand up again and acknowledge their awareness of the presence of God with the words:

> *'God always hears those who praise Him. O God, all praise be to You, O God greater than all else.'*

Next comes the humblest of all positions, the *sujud* or *sajda*. Muslims prostrate themselves upon the ground, touching the ground with their hands, forehead, nose, knees and toes. Their fingers face qiblah, and their elbows are raised and not lying on the ground. They repeat three times:

> *'Glory be to my Lord, the Most High. God is greater than all else.'*

Then they kneel up again in a sitting position known as *julus*, palms resting on the knees in a moment of silent prayer, before repeating sujud again.

There is a set number of rakahs for each prayer; the dawn prayer requires two, the zuhr and asr have four; maghrib has three and isha has four. However, many Muslims pray extra non-compulsory rakahs, following the practice of the Prophet.

At the end of the compulsory sequence they pray for all the brotherhood of the faithful, the congregation gathered there, and for the forgiveness of sins. Some Muslims can be seen sighing, and wiping their hands over their faces. When they pray for forgiveness, they place their right fist on right knee and extend the forefinger. The last action is to turn the head to right and left with the words:

> *'Asalaam aleikum wa rahmatullah'* – *'Peace be with you, and the mercy of Allah.'*

This is known as the salaam, and acknowledges not only the other worshippers, but also the attendant guardian angels.

Du'a – personal supplications

Private prayer requests are known as *du'a*. These may be said at any time. They include private thanksgivings for some blessing received (such as childbirth, passing exams, recovery from sickness and so on), requests for help, pleas for forgiveness or guidance.

Tasbih (subhah)

Sometimes worshippers carry a string of ninety-nine beads, and can be seen praying quietly while passing the beads through their fingers. These beads are called *tasbih* or *subhah*, and represent each of the ninety-nine revealed names of Allah. They are divided into three sections by larger beads. While praying, the Muslim says 'Subhanallah' ('Glory be to Allah'), 'Alhamdu lillah' ('Thanks be to Allah'), and 'Allahu Akbar' ('God is Most Great') thirty-three times, as they pass the beads.

7

THE PRACTICAL
— WORSHIP OF ISLAM —

—— Zakah – the religious tax ——

'By no means will you attain to righteousness until you spend (in the way of Allah) out of that which you cherish most.' (Surah 3:91)

The third pillar of Islam is *zakah* from the word meaning 'to purify'. Virtually every time Allah asked for the practice of regular prayer to be said by believers, He also asked for Muslims to give material help to those less fortunate than themselves. The Qur'an actually specified the categories of those people who should be helped by this giving:

'Alms are for the poor and the needy, and (to pay) those employed to administer the funds; for those whose hearts have been (recently) reconciled (to Truth); for those in bondage, and in debt; in the cause of God; and for the wayfarer; (Thus is it) ordained by God, full of knowledge and wisdom.' (Surah 9:60)

This giving is not to be considered as the sort of charity giving that is called forth by public response to tragic catastrophes in the news today. That is quite a different sort of charity, known in Islam as *sadaqah*. Zakah is a regular, sacrificial giving that depends on motives quite different from sympathy and charity.

Muslims regard everything in the universe as belonging to God, including all the things humans usually count as their own possessions or earnings. If all our belongings are only loans in trust by God, then when anything is sacrificed for the sake of God it is only being given back to its rightful Owner.

God alone has the choice of who is to be born rich or poor; therefore all Muslims have a duty towards others. The wealthy have an obligation to give; it is not a matter of personal choice for a true wealthy Muslim. When one considers one's duties in the light of one's eternal future, there is no point in clinging foolishly to possessions, or even worse, letting them become your masters.

'Those who are saved from their own greed shall be the successful.' (Surah 14:91)

'Spend your wealth for the cause of Allah, and do not be cast to ruin by your own hands; do good! Lo! Allah loves the generous.' (Surah 2:195)

Muslims have a duty to look after themselves and their families and dependants; but after that is taken care of, Allah requires that they should look at their surplus money, capital or goods, and give up a fortieth of it (or 2.5 per cent) to God's service, asking neither recompense nor thanks (Surah 26:109). This is a reasonable amount; it is not usually a massive sacrifice unless the person is extremely wealthy, and in that case, they can afford to give more. Alms are due only when the property amounts to a certain value, and has been in the possession of the person for a whole year. Alms are not due on cattle employed in agriculture, or used for the carrying of burdens.

Basically, Islam is against the idea of hoarding. All of earth's commodities, including cash, should be in use, or in flow. Any time an individual hoards something, this is disapproved of in Islam, because it is a selfish misuse of that commodity, and hoarding it is depriving others who might be able to put it to use.

Paying zakah therefore allows wealth to circulate more fairly in society, and by paying it the individual purifies himself or herself and at the same time purifies his or her wealth. It helps the Muslim to fight greed, and the recipient to fight jealousy, envy and hatred.

It is not only the poor who are helped by receiving zakah; it is also a means of helping rich people to carry out their responsibility towards others honourably, since Muslims believe that the rich person is only so by the grace of God, and his or her riches are only given in trust to them, to be used properly and not in a miserly fashion.

People giving zakah normally do it anonymously, so as not to cause embarrassment. The only time giving is done with publicity, is if that would help and encourage others to give also (see Surah 2:271). The Qur'an disapproved of people who made a show of their giving:

'Don't nullify your charity by reminders of your generosity, or by holding it against those you give it to – like those who give their wealth only to be seen by others . . . They are like hard, barren rock on which is little soil. Heavy rain falls on it and leaves it just a bare stone.' (Surah 2:264)

There is no authority to force any Muslim to pay this; it is entirely up to the conscience of the individual whether or not he or she pays it; nobody checks, and it is not a state tax even in Muslim societies – although the Muslim authorities will collect and distribute moneys when required. Therefore, zakah is very much a test of sincerity, as well as unselfishness. Being willing to pay it shows that your heart is clean of the love of money and the desire to cling to it. It shows that you are prepared to use your money for the service of humanity, and the promoting of good and justice in the world.

The Prophet (pbuh) was always very concerned for the poor and the needy, and made it quite clear that in his opinion 'he is not a believer who eats his fill while his neighbour remains hungry by his side.' (Hadith Muslim.)

—————— Sawm – fasting ——————

'O believers, you must fast so that you may learn self-restraint. Fasting is prescribed for you during a fixed number of days, so that you may safeguard yourselves against moral and spiritual ills.' (Surah 2:183–4)

The fourth pillar of Islam is to keep the fast during the ninth month of the Muslim year, Ramadan.

Ramadan is a very special time for Muslims, for it was during this month that Allah chose to call Muhammad (pbuh) to be a Prophet, and sent down the first revelations of the Qur'an. Therefore, Ramadan is seen as the most significant of months, a time of spiritual and physical discipline, and a time for making extra effort to spread love, peace and reconciliation.

Muslim fasting involves deliberately cultivating a peaceful and prayerful attitude of mind, and undergoing the physical discipline of giving up all food, liquid, smoking and sexual intercourse during the hours of daylight for the entire month. Nobody starves to death, for all these things are allowed after sunset, until the first light of the next day's dawn when a black thread can be distinguished from a white one.

It is not just a question of going without food; that is only one aspect of it, and indeed, it is not the most important aspect. Allah pointed out that if a person could not give up evil ways, violence, greed, lust, anger and malicious thoughts, He had no need of their giving up food and drink. It would be meaningless.

> *'There are many who fast all day and pray all night, but they gain nothing but hunger and sleeplessness.' (Hadith Abu Dawud)*

Tarawih prayers

Most Muslims attempt to read through the entire Qur'an in this time, and many men go to the mosque each night for prayers known as *tarawih* during which the whole text is read through. These voluntary prayers consist of either eight extra rakahs after the compulsory isha prayer (if Muslims are following the sunnah of the Prophet), or twenty extra rakahs (the practice started by Caliph Umar).

Many mosques invite special huffaz (people who know the Qur'an by heart) to lead these special prayers.

Ramadan and the seasons

As Muslims keep a lunar calendar, the Ramadan month travels through the secular calendar, coming ten or eleven days earlier each year. This means that when Ramadan falls during the winter months the fast is fairly easy, because the daylight hours are short. However, in the summer months the reverse is the case, and the fast is very strenuous indeed.

In the United Kingdom, for example, the fast in June starts at around 2 am, and finishes at around 10.15 pm on the longest days, causing considerable deprivation and suffering. (Muslims are often asked what happens in places like the Arctic Circle, the land of the 'midnight sun'. In those places, Muslims either follow the same hours as the nearest Muslims outside the polar zones, or follow the practice of Makkah, which is a 6 am to 6 pm fast.) The object of the fast is not to make people suffer, but it is intended to make them realise what it is like to go without, and to share just for a little while the deprivations of the poor, so that a more sympathetic attitude is engendered.

People excused from fasting

Any person who would undergo real suffering if made to fast is excused from doing it. This applies to people who need to be nourished, such as small children and old people, and expectant and nursing mothers. Any invalids or people whose condition would be made worse by fasting are also excused, and so are menstruating women, soldiers in battle, people on long journeys, and the mentally ill – if they cannot understand the religious reasons behind the fast. All the people in these latter categories should, however, try to make up for the fasts they have missed as soon as it becomes practicable to do so. If this is impossible, then they should donate the cost of two meals to the poor, for each fast-day they have missed, if they can afford it.

Children generally start fasting when they are quite young, perhaps just missing a dinner; they are expected to be able to take an adult role when they are around twelve years old.

A time of joy

The fast is not dreaded by Muslims, but looked forward to as a time of great joy, family celebration, entertaining of guests, and reconciliation. It is a very special month, and has a very special atmosphere for the Muslims who keep it.

When the fast starts very early in the morning, it is quite normal for Muslims to stay up during the previous night, and then go to bed after they have prayed the dawn prayer and started their fast.

In Muslim countries, where it can be assumed that the majority of people are fasting, they are sometimes woken up by a drummer, or someone firing a cannon. In the family, it is often the mother who is up and awake first, who has the job of rousing her family and getting them to take the *suhur* or early breakfast before dawn. Light nourishing foods are generally eaten at this meal, and spicy things (which make people feel thirsty) are avoided.

I'tikaf

Some Muslims go into retreat for the last ten days of Ramadan. They withdraw altogether from ordinary life and devote their entire time to prayer and reading the Qur'an. Men sometimes go to the mosque to do this, and women withdraw from normal life at home. They can only do this if they are supported by other family members who can prepare their food and so on, so the whole family feels involved.

Lailat ul-Qadr

No Muslim knows for certain which is the night of the Descent of the Qur'an, but traditionally it is celebrated on the 27th Ramadan. Scholars admit, however, that it could have been any one of the odd nights during the last ten days of Ramadan. A large number of Muslims spend this entire night in the mosque, reading the Qur'an and praying together. Indeed, the mosque is usually completely packed. Muslims believe that if they spend the whole of this night in prayer and meditation, they will be granted the blessings as if they had prayed for a thousand nights.

Breaking the fast

Although fasting makes people feel very tired and quite weak, food is prepared very carefully during Ramadan, an extra sacrifice on the part of those preparing it, who must be very tempted to eat a little. If anyone forgets, and takes a taste of something while cooking, this is not counted as breaking the fast so long as it was not done deliberately. If one sees someone doing this, it is not good manners to comment on it, or draw it to their attention. The fault is 'covered'.

As the time draws near, people feel excited, hungry, proud of their achievement. They wait for the time to end the fast, which is sometimes signalled on TV or radio, or by the call from the minaret. As soon as the sun sets, they break their fast with a sweet drink (apricot juice is a favourite) and some fruit, frequently a few dates because this was the habit of the Prophet. It is not sensible to fall upon a heavy meal and devour it without giving the stomach a little preparation first; people who do this are often sick, and regret it.

After the little meal, known as *iftar* (breakfast), the evening prayer maghrib is said, and only then will the Muslims eat the main meal. This can be quite a feast, as friends and relatives are often invited, and any poor people or strangers welcomed and included if possible. Many mosques run a communal kitchen paid for by donated money, where people may eat free. Those who are single, lonely and needy are particularly encouraged to come, and it is quite a party atmosphere.

Ramadan manners

It is considered to be very bad-mannered to eat or drink or smoke in front of a person who is fasting. In some Muslim countries people would be arrested if they did this, and even kept locked up until the fasting month was over. Some tourists in Muslim countries feel they should still be catered for, even though the people are fasting, and this can cause some problems.

General problems

People who do not fast, or who think that the Muslim fast is not particularly strenuous because they can all eat at night, often do not realise the effects it can have. The first week is often the worst, until the body gets used to the new regime. Symptoms include headaches, dizziness, nausea, light-headedness and faintness. It is especially difficult for Muslims who are addicted smokers, because they have to give up their cigarettes as well as food and drink (in fact, it is a very good time to try to kick the habit!). By the fourth week, some fasters are considerably weakened, and have little or no energy. Muslims frequently need to take rest and lie down, and because of the broken nights and little sleep, they try to catch up on some sleep during the day if possible. Muslim children at school should be· excused heavy activity, such as PE, if they cannot cope with it.

Some Muslims take an extremist point of view, refusing even to swallow the saliva already in the mouth, not cleaning the teeth or taking showers in case they swallow some water, and refusing to allow medicine or injections during the fast time. In fact Muslim tradition does allow cleaning the teeth and putting in eye drops, pointing out that saliva is already within the body and therefore does not count, and allows the taking of medicine on the grounds that a sick person is excused the fast altogether, and there is little point in actually making a person ill by deprivation of medical aid.

Benefits of fasting

Muslims maintain that there are numerous benefits to be gained from fasting. Some maintain it is a healthy time anyway, as the stomach is rested and Muslims eat more fruit and less spices than they might do normally.

Sharing food together.

However, the main benefits are spiritual and mental. First, it is excellent discipline and training in self-control. The Muslim becomes master of his or her own body and appetites.

There is a wonderful feeling of community and togetherness. Muslims are sharing an experience, and they are also sharing their food together at night. It is a particularly lovely feeling when a wealthy person can sit down with needy people, feed them and eat with them.

The fast makes people appreciate what things they do have, particularly the blessings of food and drink.

People who come from affluent societies gain at least a little knowledge of what it is like to do without. It makes them more sympathetic and understanding, and generous when they are in the position to be.

Eid Mubarrak: Muslims greeting one another after the Feast Prayer.

8

HAJJ – PILGRIMAGE
— TO MAKKAH —

*'It is the duty of all believers towards God to come to the House a
pilgrim, if able to make their way there.' (Surah 3:91)*

The fifth pillar of Islam is somewhat different from the other four, in
that it involves a complete upheaval of the individual's life for the space
of a few days. The *Hajj* (which means 'to set out with a definite
purpose') is the pilgrimage to Makkah, the 'Mother-town' of Islam,
and it is compulsory for every adult Muslim who can afford it, and who
is able to go, once in a lifetime. If any Muslim cannot afford to go, or
if it would cause hardship to their dependants, they are excused from
making the journey. Some Muslims make the Hajj many times, but this
is not encouraged nowadays because the vast number of pilgrims is
causing considerable difficulties.

Anyone who wishes to make their pilgrimage more than once is encouraged to go at some time other than the Hajj time, when the pilgrimage
is known as the Lesser Pilgrimage, or *umrah*. The true Hajj takes place
at a specific time in the Muslim calendar, in the month of Dhul Hijjah,
two months after Ramadan.

Making the Hajj used to be a considerable sacrifice and effort, some
people travelling for months and even years overland to reach Makkah.

Sometimes people save for a lifetime to make the trip, and when at
last they have enough money, they are too old or infirm to go. Any
Muslims who cannot make the Hajj are encouraged to pay instead for

another person. Sometimes a family or community will club together in order to be able to send one representative on their behalf.

Niyyah

As always in Islam, the real worship and sacrifice is of a spiritual nature rather than the physical show. If, for example, a person who had saved up for Hajj decided to donate that money instead to some unfortunate person in dire need, God would accept the *niyyah* or intention of their Hajj, and it would be counted for them as if they had done it.

People excused from Hajj

Pilgrims have to be Muslim (it is not a tourist attraction), of sound mind, and of the age of reason. They must be able to understand the religious significance of the experience. Children might be taken along with the family, but it does not count as their own Hajj until they have reached adulthood. Pilgrims have to have enough money to pay for the trip and keep up all their duty payments towards their dependants. If any person gained money to pay for the Hajj by dishonest means, it would be invalidated.

Pilgrims should also realise that they have to be reasonably fit to cope with the strenuous conditions, although many people regard it as a privilege to die on Hajj.

The Sacred Place

Makkah is regarded by Muslims as a specially holy place, and no non-Muslim is allowed to enter it. It is *haram*, which means both 'sacred' and 'forbidden'. When travellers come to Makkah by road, they will arrive at places where their passports will be checked, to make sure that they are genuine Muslim pilgrims and not just curious tourists.

——— Saudi organisation ———

The Saudi Arabian Government allocates around 300 million dollars a year to the Ministry of Pilgrimage. The new King Abdul Aziz Airport at Jiddah is the largest in the world, and the Hajj terminal takes ten jumbo jets at a time. The Saudi Government does its best to look after the vast mass of pilgrims, now numbering over two million per year. Pilgrims are organised into groups under the leadership of experienced guides. Fitting so many into the Ka'aba mosque (that only holds 75,000 at a time), and billeting them all in tents in a valley less than 2 kms wide, is no easy task!

——— Background to the Hajj ———

The Hajj pilgrimage celebrates three particular events in Muslim history. The first is the forgiveness and reunion of Adam and Eve, the second is the Prophet Ibrahim's sacrifice of his son Ismail, and the third is the life of obedience of the Prophet Muhammad (peace be upon them all).

Adam and Eve

According to the Qur'an, when Adam and Eve gave in to the temptation of Satan, they were cast out of Paradise and obliged to wander the earth in grief, hardship and pain. Not only had they lost God, they had also lost each other, and they were in great confusion and terrible unhappiness. But God had not abandoned them – He watched over them, waiting for the moment when they would turn back to Him and exchange their defiance for the desire for forgiveness. The moment they came to their senses and realised what they had done, God was able to forgive them, and they were reunited on the plain of Arafat, where there is a small hill, Mount Arafat, also known as *Jabal ar-Rahman*, the Mount of Mercy.

Muslims believe that for any pilgrim to be on that Mount of Mercy on the ninth Dhul Hijjah brings total forgiveness of all one's past sins, and enables life to begin again.

The Ka'aba

Nearby, they built a simple shrine in gratitude – the area known as the Ka'aba sanctuary. This is now the sacred shrine of Islam, the qiblah towards which all Muslims turn in prayer five times per day. The word Ka'aba means 'Cube', and it gets this name from the fact that it is a simple, cube-shaped building, some 15 metres high, built of stone blocks.

According to Muslim belief, the first shrine of the Ka'aba (also known as *al-Bait al-Haram* – the Holy House) was built by the first human, Adam, and is therefore the first shrine for the worship of God on earth.

Ibrahim and Ismail

Ibrahim was known as the Friend of God (al-Khalil), and he had vowed to sacrifice everything in his life to God, although his parents had been idol worshippers. He was a most humble and devout man, even though he was the wealthy owner of vast herds of sheep and goats. He lived peacefully with his childless wife Sarah and a second wife, an Egyptian woman called Hagar (or Hajara) who had given birth to his son Ismail. In his adult life he was tested by God, who asked him in a dream to sacrifice his dearly loved son Ismail.

(The Qur'an presents quite a different version from that of the Bible, in which it is the Prophet's younger son Isaac who was to be the sacrifice.)

Ibrahim, needless to say, did not wish to kill his dearly loved son. A stranger, who was Satan in disguise, visited him and tried to persuade him that he was being misled. Cunningly, he suggested that only the devil would ask him to do such a wicked thing. Ibrahim resisted this notion, and believed it was God's will.

Next, the Prophet's wife was tested by the devil. Didn't Ibrahim love her, and wouldn't he do anything she asked? How could she allow him to take the dream seriously? She refused to listen, and accepted God's will. Finally Ismail himself was tested. The stranger encouraged him to flee, for his father must have gone mad. He should run away, and not let himself be killed, like a fool. However, he too accepted the will of God without question.

In the end, all three of them took up stones and threw them at the unwelcome stranger, driving him away.

Ismail was so determined to submit to the will of God that he made his father place him face down, so that he should not hesitate when he saw his face. At the last moment God intervened and stopped Ibrahim, and a ram was substituted as the sacrifice. The reward for Ibrahim's obedience was that his barren wife Sarah at last gave birth to a son of her own – Isaac. (See Surah 37:100–113.)

Later, Sarah's jealousy on behalf of her son caused the family to split up and Ibrahim left Hagar and Ismail to God's care beside the ancient shrine. Here Hagar was tested again, for they were dying of thirst; but the angel Jibrail (Gabriel) appeared and opened a spring at the feet of her suffering child – the well now called Zamzam.

Later the family was reunited and Ibrahim and Ismail together rebuilt the sanctuary now known as the Ka'aba. For the last 4000 years or so the Ka'aba has always been reconstructed on the same foundations, and the faithful have gone there on pilgrimage.

The Maqam Ibrahim

In the courtyard of the mosque is a stone known as the *maqam Ibrahim*, which marks the spot where he used to stand to direct building operations.

> *'When we made the House a resort for humanity and a sanctuary, (We said): "Take as your place of worship the place where Ibrahim stood to pray." And We imposed a duty upon Ibrahim and Ismail saying: "Purify My house for those who go around and for those who meditate therein, and those who bow down and prostrate themselves."*
> *(Surah 2:125)*

The graves of Ismail and Hagar

The semi-circular enclosure in front of the Ka'aba marks the traditional site of the graves of Ismail, and Ibrahim's Egyptian wife, Hagar. (The rest of his family, and Ibrahim himself, are buried at Hebron in Palestine.)

The rites of Hajj

It is compulsory for each pilgrim to do four things on his or her Hajj. The first is to put on *ihram* clothing; the second is to perform the circling of the Ka'aba (*tawaf*); the third is to make the stand at Arafat (*wuquf*); and the fourth is to circle the Ka'aba again, after returning from Arafat.

When the pilgrim has done all these four things, he is called a *hajji* (a female pilgrim is a *hajjah*).

Ihram

Ihram literally means 'consecration', and it is a special state of holiness, expressed by three things: the complete purification of the body with full bath; the casting aside of normal garments in order to wear special clothes; and the keeping of the ihram rules of conduct.

Women wear plain, loose, full-length dresses and a head veil, so that every part of them is covered except the face, hands and feet. Men have to put on two simple pieces of white cloth, one wrapped round their waist which reaches to their ankles, and one thrown over the left shoulder. (See photograph on page 14). The object of ihram garments is both purity and equality, single-mindedness and self-sacrifice. Clothing frequently indicates rank, special career or high office; in ihram, no matter how wealthy the pilgrim or how highly born, every one is dressed the same in these simple unsewn cloths, and they stand before God as equals.

The place where it becomes obligatory to put on these garments is known as *miqat*. It is around 4 kms from the Ka'aba shrine. These days many pilgrims put on ihram even before they board their planes.

Rules of ihram

Once Muslims pass miqat, they say two rakahs, and they have really entered the state of ihram. From this moment they must not do anything dishonest or arrogant, but behave like true servants of Allah. Normal marital relations are set aside, and all flirtatious thoughts about the opposite sex are forbidden. One may not get engaged, or marry, on Hajj. To express confidence and the atmosphere of purity, and to show that all lustful thoughts have been put aside, women should not cover their faces. If any pilgrim had sexual intercourse while on Hajj, it would be invalidated.

Men must not wear jewellery or rings, and women may wear wedding rings only. No one must use perfume or scented soap (unscented soap is on sale for pilgrims). Men must leave their heads uncovered, to express their humility, but they are allowed to carry umbrellas. To express simplicity, everyone must go barefoot or in sandals that leave the toes and heels bare.

To express non-interference with nature, no one must cut hair or fingernails. To curb aggression and feel unity with God's creatures, no blood must be shed by killing animals, except fleas, bedbugs, snakes and scorpions. To develop mercy, no hunting is allowed. To feel love for nature, no plants may be uprooted or trees cut down.

Muslims strive to keep their minds at peace, and not lose their tempers, quarrel, or get exasperated by difficulties. They have to turn their minds completely to the will of Allah.

Talbiyeh

On arrival at the shrine, Muslims start reciting the *talbiyeh* prayer, a deeply moving experience as each individual among the thousands and thousands of pilgrims cries to Allah that he or she has arrived, in His service.

The words are:

> *'Labbayka, Allahumma, labbayka; labbayka, la sharika laka labbayka; innal-hamda wan-ni'mata laka wal-mulk, la sharika laka.'*

> *'At Your command, here I am, O God, here I am! At Your command I am here, O Thou without equal, here I am! Thine is the kingdom and the praise and the glory, O Thou without equal, God Alone!'*

This is the pilgrim's personal answer to the divine call to come. Some pilgrims are overcome with emotion at this point. Some shout out joyfully, and others weep.

As they enter Makkah, they pray this prayer:

> *'O God, this sanctuary is Your sacred place, and this city is Your*

city, and this slave is Your slave. I have come to You from a distant land, carrying all my sins and misdeeds, as an afflicted person seeking Your help and dreading Your punishment. I beg You to accept me, and grant me complete forgiveness, and give me permission to enter Your vast Garden of Delight.'

Tawaf

The first thing all pilgrims are required to do on arriving at the Ka'aba is to encircle it seven times in an anticlockwise direction. (They try to run for the first three circuits if they are able.) They do this, no matter what time of day or night they arrive. If they can reach the black stone (*al-hujr al-aswad*), they will touch or kiss it, or raise their hands in salute if they cannot get near. Invalids and old people are carried on specially constructed stretcher-chairs.

An example of the prayers prayed is this one, used on the fourth circuit:

'O God, Who knows the innermost secrets of our hearts; lead us out of the darkness into the light!'

At the end of the circling, they go to the Station of Ibrahim to pray two *rakahs*.

al Hujr al-Aswad

This is the famous black stone set in one corner of the Ka'aba, said to have been sent down from heaven, and probably a meteorite. There are numerous traditions about it, one being that it was originally white in colour but it turned black in sorrow at the world's sin.

It now has a silver surround, but it is still open to the touch. The deep hollow in the middle has been worn away by the millions of pilgrims who have touched and kissed it.

al-Kiswah

This is the black cloth that covers the Ka'aba shrine. It is traditionally made afresh each year in Cairo by male embroiderers. Verses from the Qur'an are embroidered around it, in gold thread. It is draped over the Ka'aba like a veil, and, like the women's veils, is lifted up

The Ka'aba and Great Mosque, Makkah.

during the Hajj. At the end of Hajj it is taken down and cut up into small pieces, which are sold off as souvenirs. Pieces are sent to mosques throughout the world, and many Muslims frame their piece and hang it on the wall as a reminder.

The Black Cloth over the Ka'aba.

Inside the Ka'aba

People rarely go inside the Ka'aba through the huge door. It has remained empty ever since the Prophet cleansed it of its 360 idols. Inside, there are no *mihrabs*, since the Ka'aba itself is the 'centre of the world' and all Muslims pray towards it. It is decorated simply, with texts from the Qur'an on the walls.

Sa'i

The *Sa'i* is the ritual of running or walking briskly seven times between the two small hills of Safa and Marwah (now a passage-way enclosed within the Ka'aba shrine). Any invalids, old people, or those who cannot walk have a special protected wheelchair path down the middle. This ritual is in commemoration of the desperate search of Ismail's mother, Hagar, for water, when she was left by the Ka'aba with her infant. It symbolises the soul's desperate search for that which gives true life.

According to tradition, when the dying Ismail scrabbled in the dust with his heels, a spring of water burst out which saved their lives, and this is known as the well of Zamzam. It represents the truth that when all seems lost, God is still present, with healing and life for the soul.

The well is still there in a chamber under the courtyard, and steps lead down to it. Pilgrims drink some of the water, and might even collect some in little bottles (these can also be bought as souvenirs). Some pilgrims dip their ihram cloths in the water intending to keep them and use them as their shrouds, when they die.

When Muslims have done both tawaf and sa'i, they have completed *umrah*, the lesser pilgrimage.

After this, male pilgrims either shave their heads, or at least cut their hair, and women cut off an inch or so of their hair. After this ey are allowed to put on their normal clothes again.

Mina

On the eighth day of Dhul Hijja, the pilgrims take a full bath and put on ihram again, and proceed to the valley of Mina some 10 kms away. This used to be a walk into the desert, but now the town of Makkah reaches virtually as far as Mina, and there are special walkways to make it easier for the huge crowds. It was in the underground walkway that there was a horrific accident with hundreds being suffocated and crushed a few years ago.

There are a few hotels in Mina, but most pilgrims stay in a huge city of tents. Some pilgrims now miss out Mina and take modern transport straight to Arafat, because of the sheer numbers involved.

Wuquf

On the ninth day, all the pilgrims have to reach the plain of Arafat (24 kms east of Makkah) and make their stand before God on or surrounding the Mount of Mercy. They have to be there between noon and dusk. Some arrive in good time, but others come rushing up from Mina, having made their dawn prayer there. If they do not arrive for the Standing in time, their Hajj is invalid.

The pilgrims' campsite in the Plain of Arafat.

This is really the most important part of the pilgrimage. The pilgrims must stand in the sweltering heat, bare-headed (the men), thinking about God and praying for His mercy. It is a time of great mystical and emotional power, and there is a tremendous sense of release – being totally wrapped in love, totally 'washed', totally cleansed.

It is an amazing sight to see over a million pilgrims perform the Zuhr and asr prayers here, especially the moments of prostration and total silence as they bow before Allah.

All the events of the Hajj after this are known as the Unfurling.

Muzdalifah

By sunset, the pilgrims begin to head back to Muzdalifah, between Arafat and Mina. There they say the maghrib and isha prayers, and collect small pebbles. They arrive back at Mina by morning of the 10th Dhul Hijja.

The jamras

Next comes the ritual of casting their pebbles at Satan, in remembrance of the temptations of Ibrahim and his family. There are three pillars set up at representative places, known as *jamras*, and pebbles are hurled at each one. While doing this, pilgrims rededicate themselves to Allah and promise to do their utmost to drive any devils out of themselves.

Stoning the *jamra* pillar

Muslims are reminded, incidentally, to be careful when hurling these pebbles, so that no one gets hurt by accident! Police are usually in attendance to keep an eye on over-enthusiastic pilgrims.

The sacrifice

After all this, on the tenth dhul hijjah, the pilgrims who can afford it buy a sheep, goat or young camel, to make their animal sacrifice. This is a three-day festival to commemorate Ibrahim's willingness to offer his son's life, but Allah making the substitution of a ram at the last moment.

Animals are expensive, and provide a huge amount of meat to be consumed, so not every person does this. The sacrificer may use two thirds of the meat for himself and those with him, and a third of it is given away to those too poor to buy their own animal. After the sacrifice the meat is roasted and eaten.

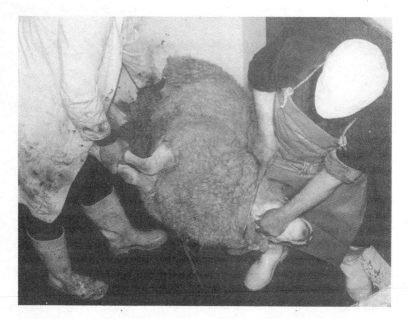

Slaughtering a sheep at Eid. The method of slaughter aims to cause the animal as little suffering as possible.

The vast number of animals slaughtered presented quite a problem until the Saudi authorities stepped in to organise the disposal of the carcases. It is impossible for all the meat to be eaten, even if it is shared, so modern technology freezes and processes all the excess meat for distribution further afield.

This is the festival known as *Eid ul Adhah*, the Major Festival (see page 94f), and at the same time as the slaughter, Muslims all over the world are making their own sacrifices to keep the Feast.

Final Rites

After this festival, male pilgrims can again shave their heads or shorten their hair, and females trim their hair again. This is done by someone not in ihram. When they return to Makkah they make the final tawaf, and then the pilgrimage is complete.

Muslim 'tourism'

Most pilgrims also take the chance to visit sites in the neighbourhood connected with the Prophet, including Madinah, where the Prophet is buried in what used to be Aisha's room (*the* hujurah), along with his friends, Abu Bakr and Umar. Nearby is the cemetery of al-Baqi where many of his family and the early Companions are buried (for example, his daughter Fatimah, his grandson Hassan and the caliph Uthman). Here one notices the extreme simplicity of the tombs, which are simply mounds of small stones. There had been grander mausoleums there in the past, but they were destroyed by the strict Islamic Wahhabi sect in the reign of King Abd al-Aziz al-Saud, who disapproved of hero-worship cults.

Pilgrims might also climb the hill Jabal al-Nur to see the cave where the Prophet received his first vision, and Jabal at-Thawr where he hid from the Makkans. They might perhaps also visit some of the famous battlefields and mosques. The Masjid at-Taqwa, built when the Prophet first entered Madinah, is interesting for having two mihrabs, one facing Jerusalem.

The Prophet said:

> *'He who comes for Hajj and does not visit me is a miser. One that comes to my grave and gives me salaam, I say salaam to that person in reply.'*

9

JIHAD

Jihad is so important a concept in Islam that it is almost regarded as a sixth pillar. It is one of the most misunderstood of all aspects of Islam. Most non-Muslims take it to mean military activity for the purpose of forcing other people to become Muslims, but this is totally against the principle of Islam, which defends individual liberties.

The fact that various rulers claiming to be Muslim have acted incorrectly, some even to the extent of horrifying brutality, does not alter this fact, any more than one could judge Christianity by the atrocities of a ruler of a Christian country, such as Hitler!

True Islamic jihad in fact insists that killing for the sake of religion is wrong. Religion should never become an oppressor. People should never be forced to accept things that they don't believe. The principle of jihad is to fight against tyranny and oppression, to bring freedom and justice and a just peace.

The word 'jihad' actually means 'striving', and in the spiritual sense, it is the constant battle against sin in all its aspects. A Muslim's real, daily striving is to be pure in spirit, and to resist evil.

Military jihad

Islam is not in favour of wars. One meaning of the word 'Islam' is 'peace'. The greeting used by all Muslims when they meet each other is '*salaam aleikum*' – 'May peace be with you.' No true Muslim can possibly regard war as a good thing (except in the circumstances to be mentioned shortly), or that it could possibly be right to inflict suffering in order to take power, food, land or anything else, by force. When this is done, it is rightly regarded as tyranny. Muslims believe that whenever a tyrant is successful, even if there is no actual fighting, there is no peace, because:

- there is no security
- people feel dishonoured and ashamed in allowing the situation to continue
- people feel frustrated and helpless, and unable to do anything about it
- people feel ashamed because they think they have acted in a cowardly manner.

In fact, the Prophet stated quite clearly that:

'If anyone walks with an oppressor to strengthen him, knowing that he is an oppressor, he has gone forth from Islam.' (Bukhari, Muslim)

Islam cannot acquiesce in wrongdoing, and this is where military jihad is sometimes the only answer. It is regarded as weak and irresponsible cowardice to ignore tyranny, or to fail to try to root it out.

'If God did not check certain people by using others, surely many monasteries, churches, synagogues and mosques would all have been pulled down. God will aid those who fight for Him.' (Surah 22:39–40)

Jihad, therefore, does not mean every single battle fought by any Middle-Eastern soldier, who may be anything from a Marxist to a member of a private bodyguard, and not a martyr for God. Many battles have nothing whatever to do with Islam. The Qur'an is quite clear on the limits that define jihad.

It should be declared only:

- in **defence** of the cause of Allah, not for conquest;
- to restore peace and freedom of worship;
- for freedom from tyranny;
- when led by a spiritual leader.
- It should only be fought until the enemy lays down arms.
- Women, children, and the old and sick, are not to be harmed, and trees and crops are not to be damaged.

Jihad does **not** include:

- wars of aggression or ambition;
- border disputes or either national or tribal squabbles;
- the intent to conquer and suppress, colonise, exploit, etc;
- forcing people into accepting a faith they do not believe.

National jihad has to be commanded by a leader who is accepted as a spiritual guide and supreme judge, who can assess the need, the cause, and give right guidance; someone not governed by personal ambition.

Sometimes after starting jihad in the correct spirit, a human leader then becomes ambitious. In this case, the qualification for leadership is lost and the community has the right to demand a change of his ways or his abdication, or even his death if he refuses to give way.

Some relevant Qur'anic teachings

'If the enemy inclines towards peace, then you must also incline towards peace.' (Surah 8:61)

'The reward for an injury is an equal injury back; but if a person forgives instead, and makes reconciliation, he will be rewarded by God.' (Surah 42:40)

'If two sides quarrel, make peace between them. But if one trespasses beyond bounds against the other, then fight against the one that transgresses until it complies with the law of God; and if it complies, then make peace between them with justice, and be fair.' (Surah 49:9)

'And hold fast, all together, to the Rope which Allah stretches out for you; be not divided amongst yourselves; remember with gratitude Allah's favour on you. For you were enemies, and He joined your hearts in love, so that by His grace you became brothers. You were on the brink of the pit of fire, and He saved you from it.' (Surah 3:103)

'Goodness and Evil cannot be equal. Repay evil with what is better, then he who was your enemy will become your intimate friend.' (Surah 41:34)

"There SHALL BE NO compulsion IN RELIGION " (Surah2 : 256)

" Fight in the cause of Allah against those who fight you, but do not attack them first. Allah does not love the aggressors".
(Surah2 : 190)

10

FESTIVALS AND
—— SPECIAL DAYS ——

The Muslim word for a festival is *'id'* or *'eid'*, from the Arab word meaning 'returning at regular intervals'. The fact that they do occur in a regular cycle is important, for it gives a repeated opportunity for renewal, to forgive enemies, put right quarrels, do things you ought to have done but have perhaps put off or forgotten, and contact people you have not seen for a long time.

Although there are several special times in the Islamic calendar, there are really only two religious festivals. These are *Eid ul-Fitr*, the feast that breaks the fast at the end of the Ramadan month, and *Eid ul-Adha*, the feast of sacrifice that takes place during the Hajj. Eid ul-Adha is the Major Festival, and Eid ul-Fitr the Minor Festival.

Both of these feasts are times of celebration and joy, at the express command of Allah as revealed in the Qur'an, when family and friends get together and the Muslim community feels a strong sense of fellowship with the whole Ummah.

——————— The aims of Eid ———————

The aims of Eid are basically to praise and thank God for His many blessings, in particular those connected with the background of the feast, and to enjoy oneself and appreciate God's blessings.

The second basic aim is unity, to arouse a heightened feeling of ummah or brotherhood. At Eid, Muslims are requested to bring loved ones to memory, particularly those who cannot be present because they live in far distant parts of the world. One should also think lovingly of all the members of the family of Islam, not just those in one's own family – whether known or unknown, rich or poor.

Equally important are loved ones who have died. Eid is a time to think about them, and say prayers for their souls.

The duties of Eid

There are several aspects to Muslim duty at Eid, all geared towards the aims of unity, peace and brotherhood. Blessings must be shared and a conscious effort made to see that no one is left lonely or depressed. The rich must share what they have (any animals sacrificed for Eid must be shared, with at least a third going to the less fortunate) and the poor must be welcomed. The lonely must not be left alone, but invited to join in either with a family or at the mosque. (Muslims have a particular responsibility to look after orphans and see that they are being loved and cared for.)

People who are not usually particularly zealous in their religion make new resolutions and put in extra effort. Those who are involved in quarrels or feuds must settle them if they are to keep the spirit of Eid.

Eid ul-Fitr

Although Eid-ul-Fitr is known as the 'minor feast', many young Muslims enjoy it more than the 'major' one, coming as it does at the end of the month-long fast of Ramadan. It is also known as *Sheker Bairam* (Turkish for 'sweet festival'), *Eid Ramadan* and *Eid ul-Sagheer* (the 'little festival'). It is little because it lasts for three days, whereas Eid ul-Adha lasts for four.

Preparations for the fast begin well in advance, as the amount of food required to feed many guests turning up for meals requires much shopping and advance cooking, usually in gargantuan quantities. Sometimes Muslim shops are so busy that they stay open all night for a few days beforehand.

Many families make decorations and hang them up, or use the tinsel trimmings more familiar to Christians as Christmas decorations. These can now be bought all over the Muslim world, and really have nothing to do with Christmas at all – they are just glittering signs of joy. Sometimes families take the opportunity to spruce up the entire house with a fresh coat of paint, or new curtains or cushion covers.

Gifts and sweets are prepared, and cards made or bought and sent out to relatives and friends. These cards usually show famous mosques, or flowers, or designs, and carry the message '*Eid Mubarrak*' ('Happy, or blessed, Feast-time').

Special contributions are collected for the poor, the *zakat ul-fitr*. This is not the same as the annual zakah, but is charity bestowed as an act of purification for the giver. Zakat ul-fitr is the equivalent of a good meal from each adult member of the family, and should be paid well before the Eid day to ensure that the poor are able to take part in the celebrations, and perhaps to buy some new clothes.

Non-Muslims in the United Kingdom may notice that the Post Office is rather more full than usual; this is because so many Muslims whose roots lie elsewhere send money to the country of their origin, to help known poor people, or to add to a particular fund. Many use the opportunity to send their annual zakah at the same time.

The announcement

The Eid depends on the sighting of the new moon, and this has caused some confusion in countries where the night sky is not always clear. If the new moon is sighted during the evening of the 29th day of the month, that night becomes the first of the new month, but if the moon is not sighted, it starts a day later, to be on the safe side. In the United Kingdom, it has not been uncommon for Eid to be celebrated on three different days, as various communities decide their date of Eid from different sources.

Many Muslims have become irritated by these differences, and feel that scientific calculations should be used to make the whole matter beyond dispute. In fact, it does not really matter as the Eid spans three days.

Traditionally, the fast is broken by the call to prayer from the mosque, or by the firing of cannons and guns, or the beating of a drum. In Indonesia, for example, the drummers are known as al-musaharati and they also wake the faithful before every dawn during Ramadan. The time is also announced on radio and TV in Islamic societies, and mosques get the news by radio, telex and telephone (if one can get through, the switchboards are so jammed at this time!).

Breaking the fast

As soon as the signal comes, there is a release of emotion and much hugging and greeting, handshaking and kissing. The fast is traditionally broken with something very simple, as was the practice of the Prophet – usually dates or other fruit, and fruit drinks or milk. A favourite drink is 'qamaruddin' (moon of religion) made by soaking apricots and dates in water for twenty-four hours.

After this simple food and drink, the family leaves the table to make the maghrib prayer. The big meal comes later.

In Muslim societies people are so excited and full of the urge to congratulate each other on completing a successful fast that they go out into the streets in party mood to wish each other 'Eid Mubarrak'. Visitors go round to call on friends and family, trying to make sure that no one is forgotten.

The Eid Day

In Muslim countries there is no work or school on Eid days – everybody has a three-day holiday. In the United Kingdom, Muslim children are granted a day off school, and sympathy from employers towards their Muslim employees is increasing. Others have to content themselves with making the early *salat ul-fitr* prayer, an hour after sunrise, and then getting on with their jobs as usual, looking forward to a good feast in the evening. Salat ul-fitr consists of two rakats with extra takbirs (saying of 'Allahu Akbar') and a sermon, usually about giving in charity. There is no call to prayer. Other Eid prayers take place in congregation between sunrise and noon.

Each person going to Eid prayer must first take a full bath or shower, and then dress in new or best clothes. They take a quick breakfast, and hurry to the Eid congregation, which may be a huge gathering in the largest mosque in the area. Sometimes the Eid prayer takes place in a park or playing field, or even a car park – any large open space where a very big crowd can gather. The congregation may consist of thousands of people, because women and children are also encouraged to attend, and traditionally mosques try to gather together to make as large an ummah as possible.

In India, Pakistan and Bangladesh, Muslims gather at the principal mosque of the city, known as the *Jami'a Mosque*. Streets become so crowded that surrounding roads are cleared of traffic. In many places there are open fields called *Eid gahs* which are used for the festival prayers.

After the prayer, everyone greets each other with 'Eid Mubarrak' and hugs and kisses, and then the round of visits to friends and family begins. Children gets lots of presents and pocket money.

At midday there is a large dinner – the first meal eaten during the day for over a month! It may have to be in several sittings if large numbers of guests arrive. Needless to say, the female members of the family will have put a great deal of effort into preparation of these huge meals. Luckily, the Middle Eastern style of cookery lends itself to these large feasts, and it is fairly easy to expand the food to fit the numbers that turn up.

During the afternoon, families often visit the cemetery to remember their beloved dead, and sit by their graves for a while.

The day ends with more visiting and entertaining, going on late into the night.

A happy celebration: Eid party.

Eid ul-Adha

This is the 'Major festival', lasting four days, and is celebrated at the end of the Hajj. It commemorates the obedience of the Prophet Ibrahim when he was called upon to sacrifice his son Ismail, and his triumph over the temptations of the devil.

Every Muslim takes part in this feast, not only the ones on Hajj. Everyone thinks about the pilgrims who have gone on Hajj, and joins with them in spirit, particularly any who have gone from their own family or community. In Muslim countries, the Hajj is reported on TV for everyone to see.

Eid ul-Adha is a serious occasion, symbolising the submission of each individual Muslim, and the renewal of total commitment to Allah. The mind is concentrated on the idea of sacrifice and self-sacrifice, symbol-ised by the actual sacrificing of a sheep, goat, cow or camel.

The animal sacrifice

In Muslim countries this does not present a problem as all Muslim men will have been trained how to slaughter an animal according to the principles of Islam. People in the West are often horrified at the thought of animal sacrifice, and regard it as cruelty and a barbaric practice. They are confusing Islamic slaughter with the ancient worshippers of idols who used to consider that their gods needed the ritual sacrifice of blood to give them strength, and so on. This has nothing to do with Islam.

> *'Neither the flesh of the animals of your sacrifice nor their blood reaches Allah – it is your righteousness that reaches Him.' (Surah 22:37)*

The creature is not slain in any way as a propitiatory sacrifice to God, but as meat for a communal feast. Any person who eats meat should be aware that the meat was once a living animal that was slaughtered specifically so that they could eat.

In fact, the Islamic principles of slaughter are to slay the creature in the kindest possible way, with the least amount of pain, and without putting the animal to fear or distress. There is sometimes controversy over whether or not halal (or 'permitted') killing is cruel or kind; Muslims maintain that it is the kindest possible method, ordained by God Himself, and that is why they do it. They do not regard killing an animal by electrocution, or by firing a bolt into its brain (normal United Kingdom slaughterhouse practices) to be kind methods at all.

Muslim slaying should be done with a very sharp knife across the jugular vein, so that the animal loses consciousness immediately. Prayers are said throughout the proceedings. Killing the animal in this way causes very little pain or distress, and the blood drains away easily.

In the United Kingdom, people must have a special licence to slaughter animals, and it is not permitted for Muslims to slaughter their own on their own premises. Licence-holders have to go to the slaughterhouse to sacrifice there on behalf of the community. When newspapers some-times print 'horror-stories' of Muslims slaughtering sheep or goats in their backyards, it is usually newcomers who are unaware of the rules or facilities provided.

——————— Dates ———————

Months in the Islamic calendar are calculated according to a lunar year, therefore each month has 29 days, 12 hours and 44 minutes; the Islamic year is shorter than the solar year by eleven days. The odd 44 minutes of the lunar month means that some years will have 355 days instead of 354. (In a stretch of thirty years, there would be eleven of these 'leap' years.) Therefore, the Islamic festival days are not seasonal, like Christian festivals, and cannot have fixed dates. Each festival comes eleven days earlier each year.

Islamic months and their
——————— special days ———————

The Islamic months are Muharram, Safar, Rabi al-Awwal, Rabi al-Akhir, Jumada al-Ula, Jumada al-Akhrah, Rajab, Shabaan, Ramadan, Shawwal, Dhu'l Qidah, and Dhu'l Hijjah. There are no special days in Safar, Rabi al-Akhir, Jumada al-Ula, Jumada al-Akhrah or Dhu'l Qidah.

Muharram

Muharram was declared the first month of the Muslim calendar by Caliph Umar. New Year's Day is celebrated after the sighting of the new moon. It commemorates the Hijra, the departure of the Prophet to Madinah, the moment that marked the turning point for Islam and the beginning of the spread of Islam. Muslims date all their years from this year, and call them AH – after the Hijra.

On New Year's Day (Muharram 1) Muslims have to 'migrate' from their past to their future, putting old sins and failings behind them and making a fresh start with new year resolutions.

10 Muharram

The tenth of Muharram, known as *Ashura*, was already a time of fasting before Islam, according to the Jewish tradition. It was originally the Jewish Day of Atonement, when the High Priest of that faith had to make sacrifices for the sins of the nation.

In Muslim tradition, this day celebrates a number of major events: the creation of the seven heavens, the land and sea; the birth of Adam; the day when Noah left the Ark after the flood to begin new life on earth; the birth of the Prophet Ibrahim and the day on which he was supposed to sacrifice Ismail; the day on which the Prophet Ayyub (Job) was released from his suffering; the day on which Allah saved Moses from the cruel Pharaoh; the day on which the Prophet Isa (Jesus) was born, and the Day on which the Day of Judgement is expected.

Fasting is not obligatory for Muslims on this day, but many do keep a day's fast. The Prophet said that anyone who fasted on this day would be granted reward equivalent to a thousand martyrdoms.

It is a particularly special day for Shi'ite Muslims (see page 24) for it marks the day when the Prophet's heroic grandson, Husain, was martyred at Karbala in the year 61 AH. Shi'ites mourn for the first ten days of Muharram, wearing black mourning clothes. On the tenth day, they perform dramatic processions led by a white horse, with floats called *tazias* depicting scenes of the events, and plays portraying the events of the suffering and death of Husain. Some of the more fervent even beat themselves with chains and cut their heads with swords, to share in a small way the sufferings of Husain.

Milad an-Nabi

12 Rabi al-Awwal is traditionally celebrated as the birthday of the Prophet (probably originally 20 August, 570 CE). There is some controversy among Muslims as to whether this day should be celebrated or not; some purists feeling it is wrong to celebrate a human being, no matter how much loved and respected. Others feel it is wrong not to commemorate the birth of such a great Prophet.

> *'God and His angels send blessings on the Prophet. O ye that believe! Send blessings on him, and salute him with all respect.' (Hadith)*

The Prophet's birthday was not observed in the early years of Islam, but was introduced by the Abbasid Caliphs of Baghdad and made popular by the Sufis in the 10th century CE. There has always been opposition to it, because it is an innovation, and it is forbidden by the strict Wahhabi Muslims of Arabia and the Deobandis of India.

However, it now has an important socio-religious function in many communities as an opportunity to remind young and old Muslims alike of what the Prophet taught and what lessons can be learnt from his life and sunnah. It is an occasion to generate love and reverence in Muslim hearts, and to send blessings on the soul of the Prophet.

Celebrations might include a procession in places with strong Sufic influence, and there are marches and meetings in Malaya. It is a public holiday in Pakistan. However, Milad an-Nabi is usually only celebrated with special meetings at the mosque to hear sermons about the Prophet's life, mission, character, sufferings and successes.

Lailat ul-Isra wal-Miraj

27 Rajab is traditionally recognised as Lailat ul-Miraj, the commemoration of the Prophet's night journey and ascent to Heaven (see page 9), eleven years before the migration to Madinah. The Prophet travelled with the Angel Jibrail on a winged animal called Buraq from Makkah to Jerusalem, and was then allowed to see both Paradise and Hell before passing on through the seven heavens to the final heaven where was the Presence of God. At that point, where he had attained the highest spiritual state attainable by humans, neither he nor the angel could go any further.

The main feature of this experience was the institution of the five daily prayers.

> *'Glory to God Who did take His servant for a journey by night from the sacred mosque to the farthest mosque whose precincts We did bless – in order that We might show him some of Our signs.'* (Surah 17:1)

Many Muslims will spend the entire night reading the Qur'an and praying. In some countries the mosques are illuminated for this night.

Lailat ul-Bara'at

This is the 'Night of Blessing', or the 'Night of the Decree', celebrated on 14 Shabaan. It is the night of the full moon before the start of Ramadan, and it was at this time that the Prophet used to begin his preparations for Ramadan by passing whole nights in prayer. Many Muslims also celebrate this night by staying awake in prayer all night. They usually visit the graves of their relatives on 15 Shabaan, and pray for the good of the departed souls.

Muslims believe that every year on this night God makes His order known to the angels as to who will live and who will die, what will be the means of livelihood for each individual for that year, and whose sins will be forgiven and who will be condemned.

Sometimes a special meal is eaten, and candles are lit. Sweets are made, and sweets and loaves distributed among the poor. Many Muslims fast for two days.

Lailat ul-Qadr

27 Ramadan is traditionally recognised as *Lailat ul-Qadr*, the Night of Power, on which the Prophet received his first revelation of the Qur'an.

> *'We have indeed revealed this (message) in the Night of Power. Who will tell you what the Night of Power is? The Night of Power is better than a thousand months. Therein came down the angels and the Spirit by God's permission, on every errand: Peace! This until the rise of the morning!' (Surah 97:1–5)*

In fact, the date is not known for certain, and Muslims may celebrate this night on any of the odd nights during the last ten days of Ramadan. Most keep the night of the 27th as an all-night of prayer at the mosque.

> *'When the Night of Power comes, Gabriel descends with a company of angels who grant blessings to everyone who is standing or sitting and remembering the Most Gracious and Glorious Allah.' (Hadith)*

Some Muslims make a religious 'retreat' (i'tikaf) for the whole of the last ten days of Ramadan.

Remembering Allah, the Most Gracious.

11

———— MOSQUES ————

Sultan Ahmad Mosque, Istanbul, Turkey.

The Muslim place of prayer is known as a *masjid* or mosque. Masjid means literally a 'place of prostration', in other words, a place where someone bows down.

This place of prayer does not have to be a special building – any clean place will do. Indeed, the Prophet said:

> *'The whole world has been made a place of prayer, pure and clean.'*
> *(Hadith Muslim)*

> *'Wherever the hour of prayer overtakes you, you shall perform it.*
> *That place is a mosque.' (Hadith Bukhari)*

In Muslim countries it is quite normal to see people praying by the roadside when it is time for prayer. It is also normal for little areas to be set aside for prayer at places like railway stations, often just a rectangular area facing the direction of Makkah, marked out by a few stones, perhaps under a tree, sometimes with a wooden board or a mat to kneel on. You might also see an arrow erected somewhere like a weather-vane, showing the direction of Makkah to the stranger.

If possible, there will be a water supply near at hand, for the ritual washing, although tayammum is acceptable for the traveller.

The mosque in the home

All Muslims pray at home sometimes; most Muslim women pray at home every time. Therefore many Muslims have a special place set aside, perhaps an entire room, which is kept clean and ready at all times, and is usually carpeted so that people can kneel in comfort. Many Muslims use little individual prayer-mats to kneel on as well as the carpet, but this is not compulsory. The prayer-mat is simply an aid to providing a clean place.

A non-Muslim visitor might find it strange that an almost empty room is regarded as the most important place in the home, but it is the heart of the Muslim home, the place of prayer.

The functions of a community mosque

Communal prayer

The mosque serves several functions. First and foremost, it is the place where Muslims gather to pray together. Mosques in the United Kingdom began with Muslims gathering together in somebody's house; and then with houses specifically bought so that they could function as mosques. Nowadays, most Muslim communities in the United Kingdom are wealthy enough to afford purpose-built centres.

Relaxation and company

The mosque is a very important part of the social life of the Muslim community. Although some Muslims are beginning to take up the culture of the West, most of them do not go to pubs or discos or other Western entertainments. Therefore, the mosque has to function as the headquarters for Muslim social life. Once the prayers are over, Muslims often stay on, chatting to their friends, and using facilities provided for activities such as table tennis and snooker.

Sometimes Muslims feel quite lonely in a non-Muslim community, and the mosque gives them a chance to meet and relax with people who speak their native language.

Most mosques also have a collection of books for study, sometimes sufficient to qualify being called a library. Muslims often invite visiting speakers and use the mosque for lectures and talks, or to discuss problems of Muslim law. The imam can use the premises if he wishes to meet people, discuss problems in the community, or help people with problems concerning their families (or, perhaps, immigration queries).

Education – the Medrassah (school)

The mosque also fulfils an important function as the school or *medrassah* where people can study the Arabic language, the Qur'an, and various Islamic subjects. All Muslims are expected to learn as much of the Qur'an as they are able, and for many this is a difficult business as Arabic is not their natural language. Classes to learn Arabic, and to study the meaning of the Qur'an (known as *tafsir*) are held every day, children usually going straight after school and studying for around two hours, five nights per week. Some schools even demand weekend work, too. Adults study at later times.

Non-Muslims do not usually realise that Muslim children are doing this, over and above their normal school studies and homework.

Boys and girls usually start these Islamic studies at the age of five; girls tend to finish at around twelve years old and boys continue until they are fifteen or so. It is quite possible to go on being a student for the rest of your life. There is an exam every year, and few children fail it. Teachers are not usually specially teacher-trained, but are willing and knowledgeable volunteers. Discipline is considered important, the duty of an adult towards a child, and adults are allowed to use corporal punishment; however, it is virtually never needed because Muslim children are respectful to their elders and behave politely.

Social functions

Next, the mosque can be hired out for all sorts of functions – meetings, parties for weddings and festival days, birthdays, circumcision parties, welcome home parties, celebrating the passing of an important exam. These are all joyful functions, and usually involve huge meals. Most mosques will have a good kitchen area as part of the complex.

Less happy gatherings are those to mourn the dead and pay the last respects to friends and relatives before burial. The mosque will have an ablutions room where it is possible to administer the last washing to the deceased before shrouding them.

—————————— **Imams** ——————————

The Imam is the leader of the mosque. There is no suggestion of priesthood in Islam, every Muslim stands before God responsible for himself or herself. However, whenever two or more Muslims come together to pray, the one with the most knowledge, or who is the older, leads the prayer.

The Imam also usually has the job of *khatib*, that is, he delivers the khutbah or double sermon at the Friday congregation, and probably organises Islamic studies for the young people. After the first sermon, the imam will sit down for a few moments, and then give the second. Then the Friday prayer of two rakahs follows, and after this people pray individually.

Any person respected by the mosque members, who has studied Qur'an and hadith, has good knowledge of the faith, and is known for his piety and common-sense can be elected Imam for the community. In the United Kingdom, each mosque elects its own Imam.

Some Imans have become famous teachers, and have rallied the faithful in times of persecution and war. The most famous Imam who has been in the news most in recent years is probably the Ayatollah Khomeini of Iran, who led the people's revolt against the Shah.

The major features outside a
————— mosque —————

Mosques can be any sort of building – many old churches and houses, and even a fire station, have been put to this use by the growing communities.

Where the mosque is purpose-built, the two most typical features are the dome and the minaret. The *dome* is an architectural device giving the impression of space and calm when one goes inside; it also helps acoustically. It is also a feature that reminds Muslims of their origins in the Middle East.

The *minaret* is a tall tower where the man who summons the faithful to prayer (known as the muezzin or muadhdhin) gives the call known as the *adhan.* Throughout the Muslim world this stirring cry is given five times per day, but in non-Muslim societies it is frequently not sounded, so as not to upset and disturb those who would not be sympathetic.

A matter that disappoints purists is that the muezzin is frequently recorded these days, and played over loudspeakers.

Regent's Park Mosque, London.

Atop the dome or the minaret one can usually see the symbol of Islam, a star cradled in a crescent moon. The five-pointed star reminds Muslims of the five 'pillars' or obligatory duties of their faith; the moon reminds them of God the Creator, and the lunar calendar which governs Islamic festivals and special days.

What to do when entering a mosque

When visiting a mosque, one should be suitably dressed. For men, this involves being clean, smart and tidy. Muslim men would not go into a mosque with shirt hanging open, or wearing shorts. For women, it is polite if they are sensitive to Muslim custom and cover the arms and legs, and wear a scarf or veil over their hair. Muslim women's dress is always modest – transparent, over-tight or too short clothing would be out of place, as would too much make-up and heavy perfume.

Both men and women should bear in mind that they will have to take off their shoes, and will probably be asked to sit down on the floor.

There will probably be two entrances at the mosque, one for men and one for women. It is normal in mosques for men and women to pray in separate areas, and how this is arranged depends on the design. Sometimes the women have a balcony, or they might pray behind a curtain at the back.

On entering the mosque, both men and women take off their shoes and place them in the rack or on the shelves provided. (If it is a very big meeting, it is sensible to keep your shoes with you in a carrier bag to avoid an irritating scramble after the prayer.) In mosques where there are a lot of tourists, it is normal for someone to be employed to look after the shoes, but they would be quite safe in small mosques.

It is not necessary to take off socks, stockings or tights, but polite people will make sure their socks are clean and not smelly or full of holes.

Muslims, who may wash their feet five times per day, are often some-what shocked by the state of non-Muslim feet!

Washing facilities

If wudu is necessary, men and women usually have separate facilities for toilet and ablutions, where there is running water.

The toilets frequently have both the flushing style, and the hole in the ground type as well, for people who are most used to coping with this sort of design. There will be several pairs of slip-ons lying around for people with bare feet to borrow. There is always water available for washing in a Muslim toilet, but there might not be toilet paper. There will either be a pipe that will automatically wash you if you are in the right position, or it is traditional to use a *loti*, rather like a jug with a curved spout, and the left hand. (The right hand is used for eating, and all 'honourable' purposes.) Outside the toilet there will be wash-basins and towels.

The most common arrangement for wudu ablutions is for a row of taps to be set in the wall over a drain, with stools arranged for people to sit on while they wash their feet.

The major features inside the mosque

The most noticeable thing straight away is the lack of furniture or decoration in the prayer room. There are no chairs or pews for people to sit on. Everyone sits on the floor.

There are no pictorial decorations or statues, because representation of this sort is forbidden in Islam as it encourages idolatry. You will never see any representation of God, angels, or the Prophets.

However, this does not mean that mosques are dull places. Many are extremely beautiful, with richly coloured carpets, different marbles for columns and surfaces, intricately patterned tiles, stained glass, beautiful chandeliers, gold-painted ceilings, ornamental calligraphy on texts from the Qur'an, and so forth.

The carpet in the prayer hall is generally marked out with lines, so that when the prayer lines form, people know where to stand and how much room to leave. The massive carpet at the Regent's Park Mosque in London has patterns marked on it rather like individual prayer-mats. However, when a large congregation comes together for prayer, they form up very close together, shoulder to shoulder, and often with one's heels touching the heels of the next person.

The Mihrab

The wall facing Makkah is known as the qiblah wall, and set in this wall is a specially decorated niche or alcove known as the *mihrab*. This is not in any way an altar, although it looks to a Christian rather like an altar area with the altar-table taken away. It simply points the direction of the Ka'aba, and concentrates the Muslim's mind upon Allah.

The prayer leader stands in front of the mihrab, which is sometimes known as the 'niche of lights', the symbol for the Divine Presence in the heart.

Some mihrabs incorporate a shell-shape; the shell symbolises the 'ear of the heart', and the pearl within is the 'Divine Word'.

The Minbar

On the right side of the mihrab is the *minbar*, the platform from which the imam gives the khutbah sermons. These can be very simple, or highly ornate. The simplest ones are usually just a couple of carpeted steps with a small platform at the top. Ornate minbars can consist of a high flight of stairs, beautifully carved and decorated.

—— How to behave in the mosque ——

Quiet, respectful behaviour is expected at all times. It is considered very bad manners to shout to someone or call out, to smoke, or to interrupt the devotions of people who have gathered there specifically for prayer.

It is also considered bad manners for Muslims to continue their meetings up to the last moment, so that people coming in to pray feel they are disturbing them.

12

SHARIAH – THE PROPHET'S WAY

'Show us the Straight Way, the way of those on whom You have bestowed Your grace, whose (portion) is not wrath, and who do not go astray.' (Surah 1:6–7)

The life and example of the Prophet is known as the Sunnah. The way of Islam, and the general title for Islamic Law is called the *Shariah*. The sunnah is known from a study of the hadith, the sayings and teachings of the Prophet, and narratives about him recorded by his friends and handed down to later generations.

Although the hadith are not part of the Qur'an revelation, nevertheless they are regarded as vitally important for the full understanding of Islam. Once, his wife Aisha was asked about the Prophet's customs and way of life. She replied: 'His way of life IS the Qur'an'.

The hadith collections

A large number of hadith collections are available today, the six major collections being Sahih Bukhari, Sahih Muslim, Sunan Abu Dawud, Sunan Tirmidhi, Sunan Nasa'i and Sunan Ibn Majah. None of these was compiled until the third century AH, so it is highly important to scrutinise how hadith were collected and kept in the very earliest of times, because there was enormous scope for inventing false sayings.

The Prophet actually disliked the writing down of his hadith, lest anyone should mistake them for the Qur'anic revelations. Once the difference was quite clear, the Prophet did not object. Abu Sa'id al-Khudri commented that what he particularly objected to were hadiths being recorded on the same piece of parchment that had Qur'an on it.

Those things the Prophet did regularly or frequently were known to every Muslim, and each generation passed the knowledge on to the next. These hadith are known as *Mutawatir,* and were narrated by such a large number of people they were obviously authentic.

—— The importance of checking ——

The Prophet's disciples used to make a conscious effort to memorise his sayings accurately. Anas b. Malik, the Prophet's nephew, for example, said that he and his companions used to sit in a circle to recount hadith to each other from memory; sometimes as many as sixty people joined these circles. One disciple (Ata b. Abi Rabah) commented: 'Whenever we left after meeting Jabir b. Abdullah, we used to repeat the hadith that we heard from him. Abu al-Zubair was the best among us at remembering them'.

This gives an idea of how the first hadith were learnt, recorded and passed on. Abdullah b. Masud said: 'Remind each other often, because that is the purpose (of hadith)'.

The Prophet gave a very stern warning to those who might be tempted to make things up or exaggerate:

> *'Whoever intentionally ascribes to me what I have not said, then let him occupy a place in Hell-fire.' (Bukhari)*

The Companions were prepared to go to enormous lengths to check out hadith. Abu Ayyub Ansari once travelled all the way from Madinah to Egypt just to hear from Uqbah b. Amir's own lips the words of the one hadith which had very important implications: 'Whoever conceals a Muslim (i.e. covers his sins), Allah will conceal him on the Day of Resurrection.' When he had checked it out, he set off home without even entering the house. Al-Bukhari reported that Jabir b. Abdullah once undertook a month-long journey to Syria to hear a single hadith.

By the third century AH there was a vast amount of material running to tens of thousands of hadith to scrutinise, and scholars selected a limited number in their compilations, incorporating earlier material. They developed very strict rules for deciding whether a hadith was *sahih* (authentic), *da'if* (weak), or *maudu'* (doubtful).

The collection by Imam Muhammad b. Ismail al-Bukhari (d.256 AH), is regarded as the most authentic. This is a collection of 7563 hadith, covering a vast range of subjects. The second most important collection is that of Muslim b. al-Hajjaj (d.261 AH) containing 7422 hadith. It is easier to read than al-Bukhari's collection because it arranges all the sayings relevant to one issue together.

The collection of Muhammad b. Yazid b. Majah (d.275 AH) contains 4341 hadith, and that of Abu Dawud Sulaiman b. Ash'ath (d.275 AH) contains 5266.

——— Weak and suspect hadith ———

The chain of transmitters was always carefully scrutinised for authenticity. It would be very difficult to ascertain the authenticity if a writer mentioned a hadith without giving its source.

It is unfortunately a well-known fact that false hadith were soon in circulation, however pious the intentions of those who fabricated them; there is a record of one such fabricator being executed for inventing some 4000 false hadith!

It is also commonplace to read numerous very weak and highly suspect hadith in countless Muslim articles and publications, often copied, nowadays, from one modern article to the next, without the least concern for scholarship or the veracity of the hadith. This has done considerable damage to the image of Islam in academic circles.

Is keeping the Sunnah
—————————— compulsory? ——————————

The vast majority of Muslims would never go against the teachings of the Prophet as recorded in the hadith; but occasionally reformers or people wishing to 'update' Islam take the point of view that it is enough to study the Qur'an, and that if Allah had wished a thing to be known or done, He would have certainly included it in the Qur'an and not left it to chance.

This attitude is fairly common among those who regard the study of Shariah to be an enormous burden, for the amount of hadith material and subsequent scholarly opinion upon it is enormous.

The Prophet himself was well aware that this would happen, and gave clear warning against it:

> *'I have indeed been given the Qur'an and something similar to it besides it. Yet, the time will come when a man leaning on his couch will say: "Follow the Qur'an only; what you find in it as halal, take as halal, and what you find in it as haram, take it as haram." But truly, what the Messenger of Allah has forbidden is like what Allah has forbidden.' (Hadith Abu Dawud and Darimi)*

The argument against trying to abandon study of the hadith is emphasised in the Qur'an itself:

> *'O you who believe! Obey Allah and obey the Messenger, and those charged with authority among you; and if you differ in anything among yourselves, then refer it to Allah and the Messenger.' (Surah 4:59)*

Another famous passage reinforcing the Prophet's authority is:

> *'Take whatever the Messenger gives you, and keep away from what he forbids you.' (Surah 59:7)*

The Prophet specifically stated:

> *'Behold, I have left among you two things; you will never go astray so long as you hold fast to them – the Book of Allah and my sunnah.' (Hadith Hakim)*

The difference between Din and ——————— Shariah ———————

The Shariah is the detailed code of conduct or the canons comprising ways and modes of worship, standards of morals and life, laws that allow and prescribe and that judge between right and wrong. The *Din* is the faith of Islam, which undergoes no change whatsoever. But the matters of shariah are frequently amended, according to the needs of the time and the society.

Behaviour is divided into five categories: *fard* or *wajib* – things which are compulsory and *must* be done, such as keeping the five pillars; *haram* – things which are forbidden and should never be done, such as committing adultery or eating pork; *mandub* or *mustahab* – actions which are recommended but not compulsory, such as making extra voluntary prayers; *makruh* – actions which are not actually forbidden, but are disliked or disapproved of, such as divorce; and *mubah* – actions which have to be decided by conscience because there is no clear guidance. Most problems pertaining to modern life fall in the mubah section. Whatever is not actually forbidden in Islam is permitted, under the guidance of Islamic principles and conscience.

——————— Ijtihad, qiyas and ijma ———————

How can a law laid down fourteen centuries ago in the Middle East meet all the complex demands and pressures of modern technological civilisation? How can anyone know whether it is right or wrong to watch TV, play pop music, use birth control, etc?

Working out Muslim principles is called *ijtihad*. This means individuals use modern reason and judgement to decide on the course of action most in keeping with the spirit of Qur'an and hadith.

Decisions made in this manner are called *ijma*, or consensus. However, consensus does not mean the opinion of the masses, or even the collective opinion of rulers of a Muslim country. Even if they passed a law unanimously, if it contradicted the principles of Qur'an and Sunnah, it would be regarded as anti-Shariah and rejected by true Muslims. Ijma refers to the collective judgements of the learned Muslim teachers –

the *ulema*. But even these are not regarded as totally binding (like a Qur'anic command), since they are based on human opinions. The only ijma accepted as binding are those ancient ones made by the first caliphs, who had been the Prophet's closest companions.

In making decisions, account must always be taken of the opinions of respected people, present and past; previous decisions and the reasons for them; the general sense of justice; concern for the public good; and a most practical consideration that is sometimes overlooked by ambitious leaders and politicians – the acceptance of the masses. *Qiyas* means analogical reasoning, using past analogies with their decisions as precedents in each new situation.

The principles behind Shariah deter any pressure groups – even highly religious ones – from imposing burdens and duties on people which go beyond the spirit of Islam, and become tyrannical.

Fiqh

The technique for working out Shariat law is called *fiqh* from the word for 'intelligence' or 'knowledge'.

Fiqh is detailed law derived from the Qur'an and hadith, covering the myriad of problems that arise in normal everyday life. In the earliest times a large number of scholars applied themselves to this study, but four major schools (known as *madhhabs*) emerged in Sunni Islam, and still remain. They are named after the most eminent jurists of that early period – Imam Abu Hanifa, Imam Ahmad ibn Hanbal, Imam Malik and Imam Shafi'i. The Shi'ite sect of Islam follow an earlier school, that of Imam Ja'far al-Sadiq – the teacher of Abu Hanifa.

Sunni and Shi'ite Muslims differ in their beliefs of who is permitted to interpret Shariat law. The Shi'ites believe that living religious scholars, known as *mujtahids*, have an equal right to interpret Divine Law as those scholars of the past. They also believe that there was a time when the spiritual leadership of the world depended on the descendants of the Prophet's daughter Fatimah, and these imams had the right to exercise ijtihad freely. (Leading imams earned the title ayatollah or 'shadow of God', and the most famous modern one was undoubtedly Ayatollah Khomeini of Iran, now deceased.)

Tasawwuf

Whereas Fiqh deals with the apparent and observable conduct – the actual fulfilling of duties – *Tasawwuf* is concerned with the spirit behind it. For example, when saying prayers, the performing of correct ablution, facing Makkah, the times the prayers are said and the number of rakats performed are all matters of fiqh; whereas the intention, concentration, devotion, purification of soul, and effect of prayers on our morals and manners are matters of tasawwuf. Fiqh governs the carrying out of commands of the minutest detail; tasawwuf is the measure of the spirit of obedience and sincerity.

It has been said that a worshipper devoid of spirit, although correct in procedure, is like a handsome man lacking in character; and a worshipper full of spirit but defective in performance is like a noble man deformed in appearance.

'God speaks to the heart.'

13

—— SUFISM ——

'Go sweep the chamber of your heart. Make it ready to be the dwelling-place of the Beloved. When you depart out, He will enter it. In you, empty of yourself, He will display all His beauty.' (Shabistari)

Sufism, or *Tasawwuf*, is Islamic mysticism. As a movement, it developed as a reaction against dry Islamic legalism, but it has always played a fundamental part in the religious experience of those Muslims (like the Prophet himself) who devoted themselves to a lifetime of prayer and closeness to God. Although many non-Sufi Muslims are suspicious of it, it cannot be separated from Islam, for it is basically the 'awakening of the heart' by means of submission.

Some Muslims regard it as the most important aspect of Islam, whereas those, who distrust the emotional and intuitive side of religious experience (with its obvious scope for abuse and ego-tripping), relegate it virtually to the sidelines. It depends on what type of person the Muslim is. Sufism has been called the heart or spirit of Islam by those who grasp its value; but it is regarded with suspicion by Muslims who base their faith on obedience to the correct ritual performance of Islam, and who fear *bida* (innovation).

—— Wool ——

The name 'sufi' may come from the Arabic *suf* meaning 'wool', in which case it refers to their simple garments of undyed wool. The basic wool robe was worn as a sign of ascetic living, of giving up the luxuries of life – food, dress and shelter – and accepting simplicity and poverty.

An English Naqshbandi Sufi at Peckham Mosque.

Another possible origin of the word is from the Greek *sophos* which means 'wisdom'. Others think it comes from the root *safa* which means 'purity', or from the verb *safwe* to mean 'those who are chosen'.

Aims and goals

Sufis have many aims. Basically, they are:

- to abandon the desire for worldly wealth and luxury;
- to search for an inner, spiritual life;
- to 'purify the heart' and achieve union with God, with direct emotional experience;
- to become so close to God that human consciousness becomes totally lost and absorbed in consciousness of God; and
- to overcome the appetites and desires of the human body with its concern for self.

Ali said:

> *'Ascetism is not that you should not own anything, but that nothing should own you.'*

Conflict with rulers

Sufism encourages renewal, revival and militancy in the hopes of restoring the pure and original message of the Prophet, with the placing of leadership in the hands of those who are closest to emulating the way of life of the Prophet. The ruler should be the most qualified person in spiritual terms, the most evolved in consciousness, pious, humble, and accessible to the people – not someone who lives in arrogance, contempt and luxury, and who (frequently) terrorises the people. This, obviously, is a great threat to the decadent and extravagant lifestyle of many so-called 'Muslim' rulers.

——— Conflict with orthodoxy ———

During the ninth and tenth centuries the jurists began teaching Islamic jurisprudence in a more formal and standardised manner, and the Sufis saw their role as keeping the spirit and full meaning of Islam alive rather than adhering to the formal and ritualistic aspect of the 'State' religion which was ominously taking shape.

Some Sufis, however, adopted so outspoken and ecstatic a lifestyle that they attracted a notoriety which really set them apart from orthodox Islam. Their claims that their souls had merged with God had overtones of shirk; furthermore, music, chanting, dancing or recitation of poetry were increasingly used in order to induce transcendental experiences, and these were not practices encouraged by orthodox Islam.

Jalal ud-Din Rumi
——— (the Mevlana of Qonya) ———

The thirteenth century is usually regarded as the golden age of Sufism, and its chief exponent was Jalal ud-din Rumi of Qonya, (1207–73) who founded the order of whirling dervishes. These sought ecstasy through gyration accompanied by music that was intended to represent the order of the heavenly spheres.

Acceptance of God's will, whatever it might be, was the highest form of sacrifice of self, the highest proof of love. The Mevlana taught that one should not ask for personal requests in prayer, but should strive to be content. This was pure Islam, pure submission. Love was what mattered, not knowledge, or greatness or striving. To achieve love meant understanding unity, God's light shining into all the dark places of the earth and making them one.

Some of the Mevlana's famous sayings

'God speaks to everyone . . . He speaks to the ears of the heart, but it is not every heart which hears Him. His voice is louder than the thunder, and His light is clearer than the sun, if only one could see and hear. In order to do that, one must remove this solid wall, this barrier – the Self.'

'There are many roads to the Ka'aba . . . but lovers know that the true Holy Mosque is Union with God.'

'The sun lights up a thousand courtyards. Take away the walls, and you will see that it is all the same light.'

'You belong to the world of dimension, but you come from the world of non-dimension. Close the first shop and open the second.' (Rumi)

Tariqas

The Sufi science of self is called a *tariqah* ('Way' or 'path'). All Sufis claim a chain or linkage or revelation (called the *silsilah*) which goes back to the Companions and to the Prophet himself. There were two kinds of membership: the initiates (or inner circle) and the associates (who attended occasionally). Any initiate on a particular path was known as a *murid*, a disciple who owes absolute allegiance to his or her particular *shaikh*. This close relationship with the shaikh is a vital part of Sufism, and a dying shaikh usually elects his successor (if a suitable person is available), to whom obedience and loyalty is transferred.

Zawiyahs

Zawiyahs (or Khaneqahs) are places of spiritual learning and concentration where Sufis meditate and remember God, and train their disciples. They are also known as tekkes in Turkey, and ribats in North Africa. They are centres of missionary work, and frequently the shaikhs associated with the particular tariqa are buried there. To this day, they are visited by thousands of pilgrims. Examples are the famous shrines of Abdul Qadir Gilani in Baghdad, Muinuddin Chisti in Ajmeer, India, Shah Halal in Sylhet, Bangladesh, Jalaluddin Rumi in Qonya, Turkey, and Shams-i-Tabriz in Multan, Pakistan.

Sufi Orders in the UK

The two main Orders of Sufis practising in the UK today are the Naqshbandis and the Murabitun. The Naqshbandis follow the Turkish Shaikh Nazim, who is the 40th shaikh in line from Abu Bakr. Their UK headquarters is at Peckham Mosque, South London. The Murabitun follow the Scottish Shaikh Abd-al Qadir. Their headquarters is in Norfolk. Both tariqas have followers all over the country.

The important role of Sufism

Many people consider that Sufism saved Islam from being over-influenced by 'legalism', for there is always a temptation for Muslims without comprehension to relegate Islam merely to observance of rules and ritualism, as if that would be sufficient for salvation. Sufis fought to keep the love of God and the Prophet alive. Their humility, sincerity and devotion, character and conduct had a great impact on those who observed them.

However, Sufis have frequently been misunderstood, and frequently persecuted. For these reasons, they have sometimes gone 'underground' in order to safeguard and continue their teaching discreetly, either through fear of tyrannical rulers, or of the power-mongering religious scholars who felt that their religious authority and position in society were being challenged and undermined by the popularity of the Sufis.

They were and are the champions against materialism, and still play an important part wherever rule-keeping, rather than movement of the spirit, threatens to take over the Ummah.

Their influence within Muslim nations remains enormous, and it is rare to find a Sunni Muslim ruler who is not affiliated to one or other of the Orders.

14

—— HUMAN RIGHTS ——

Many people seem to spend a great deal of their time and effort demanding their rights, and are frequently discontented whatever they receive. In Islam, rights are not an end in themselves, but the means to fulfil the duties of life. The human being who is worthwhile contributes to life and shares in the service of humanity, alleviating human suffering and working hard to take care of those in his or her charge. The true Muslim is interested in the economic and scientific advancement of humanity, as well as moral and spiritual well-being.

—————— Moral awareness ——————

It is moral awareness and participation in the good of society that makes a human being different from an animal, and was the aim of Allah in ordaining humans as His khalifas on the planet.

'Do you think that We created you for nothing, or that you would not return (and give account)?' (Surah 23:115)

Humans are granted the right to life in order to use it in the production of good works and deeds. They have free-will to behave as they choose, but when they choose to submit to the will of God, they strive to pass their lives in the best way possible.

'Each of you is a shepherd, and each is responsible for his (or her) flock.' (Hadith Bukhari)

Consciousness of these duties drives the Muslim to strive to uphold the rights of the oppressed by strengthening the legal and social foundations of society and by countering those who trample on the rights and dignity of others. Any so-called Islamic government that has itself become a tyrant has departed from the principles of Islam, no matter how self-righteous it might claim to be.

The basic human rights

All human beings are the creations of God, and loved by Him. Therefore there are certain basic rights which should be shared by the whole of humanity, whether people are Muslim or not. All have the right to be fed, clothed, educated and cared for by the society which governs their existence.

Every society contains people whose disabilities prevent them from working, or who are too sick or too weak to earn sufficient wages to secure a decent life. There are children who have lost parents, wives who have lost husbands, old people who are no longer able to care for themselves. Any society with the least respect for human dignity would not allow such people to be left neglected and uncared for.

Islamic obligations

Islam makes it obligatory for the wealthy and able-bodied to support the less fortunate. No society should victimise or terrorise its weak members, or deprive people of liberty for no reason. No society should try to 'brainwash' its members, or attempt to force them to believe things against their natural will, ability or awareness.

These human rights have all been granted by God Himself, and not by any ruler or government, and it is the duty of Muslims to protect these rights actively. Failure to do so results in the loss of these rights, and leads to *tughyan* – tyranny and suffering.

> *'He will not enter Paradise whose neighbour is not secure from his wrongful conduct.' (Hadith Muslim)*

> *'None of you is a true believer until you wish for your brother what you wish for yourself.' (Bukhari and Muslim)*

—— Specific human rights in Islam ——

In Islam, human rights include the following specific areas:

(i) The right to life.

(ii) The right to equality.

(iii) The right to freedom.

(iv) The right to freedom of opinion.

(v) The right to political freedom.

(vi) The right to emigration and refuge, to remove oneself from trouble and oppression.

(vii) The right to work and provide for oneself and one's family.

(viii) The right to justice.

(ix) The right to equality before the Law.

(x) The right to protect one's honour.

(xi) The right to social welfare and the basic necessities of life.

(xii) The right to marriage.

(xiii) The right to privacy, and security of private life.

(xiv) The right to dignity, and not to be abused or ridiculed.

(xv) The right of education.

(xvi) The right to protest against tyranny.

(xvii) The right to freedom of expression.

(xviii) The right to freedom of association.

(xix) The right to freedom of conscience and conviction.

(xx) The right to protect religious sentiments.

(xxi) The right to participate in affairs of state.

(xxii) The right to rise above the level of animal life.

There are numerous passages in the Qur'an and hadith expressing people's rights:

'Why should you not fight in the cause of Allah and of those who, being weak, are ill-treated and oppressed? Men, women and children, whose cry is: "Our Lord, rescue us from this town whose people are oppressors, and raise for us one who will protect and help us!"' (Surah 4:75)

'How are rights neglected? When sins are committed openly, and no one prevents the sinners from wrongdoing.' (Hadith Targhib)

'He who amongst you sees something abominable should modify it with the help of his hand; and if he has not the strength to do that, then he should do it by word of mouth; and if he has not the strength enough for that, then he should at least (abhor it) from his heart.' (Hadith Muslim)

– The useful guide of the conscience –

The conscience is the guide to the Muslim, and should always be listened to, for it brings the stirrings of Allah's will. The Prophet accounted a person a believer 'when your deed pleases you and your evil deed grieves you'. He was then asked what sin was, and replied: 'When a thing disturbs your heart, give it up.' (Hadith Ahmad).

Moreover, the Prophet had no time for hypocrisy. He said:

'Look at your own faults. This will prevent you from finding faults with others. Never be in search of the faults of others. It is sinful on your part to detect those faults in others which exist in you.'

15

THE SANCTITY
OF LIFE

'Allah decrees the time span for all things. It is He Who causes both laughter and grief; it is He Who causes people to die and to be born; it is He Who causes male and female; it is He Who will recreate us anew.' (Surah 53:42–47)

Life is the most precious of all the responsibilities that God has granted to any living creature. Muslims believe that no human has an automatic right to life – it is God's gift. If God wills otherwise, that person will cease to be, or will not be granted life in the first place. It is God's prerogative.

The time span

The human body is part of the world of matter, but the individual soul is God's 'loan' to that body, for so long as He wishes; it is in a sense a visitor, a guest. Moreover, God knows the exact length of the individual's lifetime, even before his or her conception.

Just as the decision to grant life is God's prerogative, so is the time span for that life, and the ending of the soul's occupation of the body. Muslims believe it is gross presumption for any human to try to interfere with that decision, no matter how well meaning, or even to try to find out when it will be. That is not a matter granted to human knowledge.

———————— Gratitude and hope ————————

Muslims should be grateful to Allah for their life, whatever the circumstances in which they are born, or whatever hardships they may have to face. But they should never forget it is God's gift, and it is a Muslim's duty to live every day so that they are ready to hand their life back with easy conscience, should God demand it.

It is when facing death that a believer has a great advantage over a non-believer, for the peace of mind and hope that it brings. The choice of whether or not to believe in life after death is one of the freedoms granted to humans during their earthly life; that freedom no longer exists after the moment of death, because they are confronted with the new situation, and must cope with it as best they can.

All humans must die, and it is pointless and futile to resent the inevitable end of the human body.

> *'When your time expires, you will not be able to delay the reckoning for a single hour, just as you cannot bring it forward by a single hour.'*
> *(Surah 16:61)*

Muslims believe it is a foolish gamble to assume that all God's messengers who have taught of the life to come have been misled by God.

> *'Do you think that We shall not reassemble your bones? Yes, surely, yes – We are able to restore even your individual fingerprints.'*
> *(Surah 75:3–4)*

Many people desperately try to prevent their deaths and pray for Allah to grant them some miracle that will keep them alive, but Nature runs its course and miracles are not granted. On the other hand, many people long to die, because they are so unhappy or in such pain, but Allah requires them to go on living.

Suicide

Since every human soul has been created by Allah and is owned by Him, no person is allowed to damage or attempt to kill any body in which it is the 'guest'. To kill yourself is just as forbidden as to kill any other person unlawfully. People who commit suicide are presumably very depressed and beset by problems that seem to have no answer. But to kill oneself is no escape whatsoever, for the torments suffered in increased awareness after death are much greater than what they endured while still living – for now they realise who really loved them, and experience the hurt of those left behind, while being able to do nothing to alleviate their awful pain.

> *'He who kills himself with sword, or poison, or throws himself off a mountain will be tormented on the Day of Resurrection with that very thing.' (Hadith Muslim)*

Life may be full of hardships, sufferings and loneliness, but Muslims are taught to accept these as part of their test, and to face them with patience and humility, and not lose faith.

> *'None of you should wish for death for any calamity that befalls you, but should say: "O Allah! Cause me to live so long as my life is better for me, and cause me to die when death is better for me."' (Hadith Abu Dawud)*

Of course, nearly all people who commit suicide do it as the result of mental illness, or when the balance of their mind is disturbed. It is important to realise that such people are not counted as responsible for their actions, and are forgiven by God, in His compassion.

> *'There are three (sorts of people) whose actions are not recorded; a sleeper until he wakes, a (person with) disturbed mind until he is restored to reason, and a child below the age of puberty.' (Hadith Abu Dawud)*

Shariat Law concurs that if any people in these categories commit crimes they will not be punished, and if they sign contracts they will not be binding; if they commit suicide while in this state, they are not held responsible for their actions.

However, deliberate and calculated suicide is considered a total lack of faith in God and a terrible sin. It is an extremely rare occurrence in Islam, for a genuine Muslim would not even consider it.

Euthanasia

Sometimes a person's life seems such a burden or so painful that well-meaning people consider it would be better to end it. Just as one would not stand by and see an animal suffering, but would put it out of its misery, so they consider euthanasia (a 'good death') for humans, to end their sufferings. Euthanasia is usually thought of as being 'put to sleep' painlessly, perhaps by drug overdose.

Many hospital cases are considered hopeless, and doctors may decide that to keep on trying more and more drastic measures to keep the patient alive is pointless, and only prolonging their suffering. In these cases, the notice 'NTBR' ('Not to be resuscitated') appears on their medical sheet, the doctors taking the point of view that it is better to let nature take its course, and that they 'should not strive officiously to keep alive' when to continue fighting for that life only causes increased distress.

Some people consider that putting a gentle and easy end to human life should be considered when an infant is born terribly deformed or mentally ill, when the prospective lifetime in front of it would be grim. It seems kinder to the child and to the family that loves it.

Others consider that it would be kinder to put an end to old people when they become 'vegetables', or to anyone who has been in a coma for a long period. If everybody in a coma was kept alive indefinitely, there would be a lack of hospital beds for 'ordinary' patients.

These dilemmas are faced every day by doctors called upon to 'play God'. All these matters are highly emotive, and it is one thing to discuss examples and issues, and quite another to be requested to end a person's life.

Muslims reject euthanasia, because the reason for the disability or suffering will be known to God, and 'mercy killing' does not usually allow the individual to be killed any choice in the matter. They find the thought appalling that anyone should be put to death out of social convenience. Our tests may indeed seem unfair to us when we do not know the reasons, but Allah knows, and He is never unfair.

The Muslim attitude is to bear personal tragedies with love and fortitude, and to make life as comfortable as possible for the suffering person.

Capital punishment

'The law of equality is allowed for you in cases of murder.' (Surah 2:178)

'Do not take life, except for just cause. If anyone is wrongfully killed, We give his heir the right to demand retribution or to forgive; but let him not exceed bounds in the matter of taking li' (Surah 17:33; 5:68)

In Islam there are three crimes which are considered 'just cause' for giving the death penalty – murder, publicly committing adultery (see page 129) and openly attacking Islam in such a manner as to threaten it, having previously been a believing Muslim.

In the case of murder, Islam accepts the justice of taking a life for a life, although individuals are not allowed to take the law into their own hands in seeking revenge. The execution of a murderer should only take place after a proper legal trial, which fully examines the state of the murderer's mind, and so forth. The Prophet also granted the heirs of the murdered person the right to forgive the murderer, or to accept money compensation, and preferred it if they could find it in their hearts to forgive.

As regards the death penalty for attacking Islam, this does not mean that Muslims are condemned to death if they forsake the faith. Belief can never be imposed on a person. Even though many religious people commit the sin of trying to force others into belief, this is totally against the command of Allah who stated:

'Let there be no compulsion in religion.' (Surah 2:256)

The crime that merits the death penalty in Islam is actively turning on the Ummah and endangering and betraying it. Any insults a person offers to God are a matter between God Himself and that person; and Muslims cannot demand a death penalty for those who attack them who have never been Muslims, and who do not understand the goodness of a way of life truly submitted to God's will. However, it seems reasonable to Muslims that if someone has genuinely been a member of the faith and then deliberately attacks its members and endangers them, that person must be really twisted and corrupt, and worthy of the sentence of death unless they repent. However, repentance and reconciliation are far better to restore the unity of the Ummah:

'Believers are like the parts of a building. Each part supports the others.' (Hadith Muslim)

'If any single part of the body aches, the whole body feels the effects and rushes to its relief.' (Hadith Muslim)

'Believers are a single Ummah, so make peace and reconciliation, and fear Allah, that you may receive mercy.' (Surah 49:10).

Abortion

'Do not slay your children because of poverty – We will provide for you and for them.' (Surah 6:151)

Islam permits birth control, so long as both mother and father are aware of it, provided the method is one which prevents a woman conceiving in the first place. They do not allow abortion of an unwanted foetus, except in the case where a mother's life would be put at risk, in which case the *actual* life of the mother takes precedence over the *potential* life of the unborn child.

As regards abortion, there are two schools of thought regarding terminating pregnancy in its early stages. Some Muslims argue that the soul does not enter the foetus until it 'quickens' at around the 16th week, and therefore if an abortion was absolutely necessary, it could be performed before that time.

Others maintain that no one really knows what the soul or spirit is, and when the Prophet was asked to define it he was instructed by Allah to say that knowledge of it belonged to God alone. Therefore the foetus represents a potential life from the moment of conception, and should be protected and given all the rights of human life.

The usual practice of birth control among the Arabs before the time of the Prophet was to bury newborn infants (generally girls) face down in the sand before they drew breath. This practice was totally forbidden in the Qur'an:

'Slay not your children . . . the killing of them is a great sin.' (Surah 17:31)

Therefore, under the Shariat principle of analogy, it is also forbidden to kill babies or foetuses by other methods.

Some women argue that it is a woman's right to decide what she does with her own body, conveniently forgetting the rights of her unborn child's body. The Qur'an reminds these mothers that on Judgement Day these infants will require to know why they were killed.

'When the souls are sorted out, when the female infant buried alive is asked for what crime she was killed . . . when the World on High is unveiled . . . then shall each soul know what it has sent ahead.'
(Surah 81:7–9, 11, 14)

Islam teaches that all human beings are loved by God.

16

JUSTICE, CRIME AND PUNISHMENT

'O believers, be staunch in justice, witnesses for God, even though it be against yourselves, your parents or your kindred, whether the case be of a rich person or a poor person – for God is nearer to both (than you are); so do not follow passion, lest you lapse (from truth), and if you lapse or fall away, then lo! God is ever informed of what you do.' (Surah 4:135)

In Islam, all people are equal before the law, and no citizen should be beneath the protection of the law, no matter how humble. Every citizen should have equal rights, including the right of defence if accused of something. No citizen should ever be above the law, no matter how powerful, rich or influential. If any person can buy his or her way out of a rightly deserved punishment, then that society is corrupt and should be challenged.

— The importance of Islamic judges —

When true Islam governs justice, a judge should be above corruption and bribery, or fear of the power of his prisoner. Moreover, Shariat law stipulates that the judge who tries the case should not do so while he or she is angry, hungry, restless, or absorbed in some other matter. Accused people should not be treated as criminals before they have been proved guilty, and the case against them confirmed. No one should ever be imprisoned unless they have been properly convicted of a crime by an unbiased court. No one should be threatened, punished or imprisoned because of the fault of others, or to intimidate others.

Shariat law is always carried out publicly, not for the sake of brutality or to please a bloodthirsty audience, but because it is vital that justice is seen to be done, and that the bounds are not exceeded. Muslims cannot approve of trials and punishments being carried out in secret, with the possibility of inhumane treatment and torture.

——— Is Islamic law barbaric? ———

Many people in the West feel that Islamic justice is cruel and barbaric, requiring numerous executions, floggings, and mutilations. Such things as public beheadings and people having their hands amputated always grab the headlines, and horrify a public that has grown accustomed to a society in which criminals can be treated very leniently by the legal system, and children in school grow up with teachers forbidden to administer corporal punishment.

Two comments have to be made. Firstly, many of the things regarded as 'Islamic' are not in the least Islamic, but are the actions and culture of rulers and governments that may well govern Islamic people, but who flout the laws of Islam and may actively go against them. Islamic law, when properly interpreted and carried out, is always merciful and not barbaric. Unfortunately, it is frequently abused or misinterpreted by people with a variety of motives (including a tyrannical zeal for an extremist form of Islam which is not sunnah).

Secondly, one must comment that in truly Islamic societies there is virtually no drunkenness with its associated catalogue of crimes; no theft; no adultery or sexual freedom with its accompanying distress and consequences; no battering of children or old people; no cheating or swindling. It seems impossible in this day and age, but those who have known life in real Islamic society always come away impressed by the lack of criminality and lawlessness.

Of course, many Muslim areas, frequently the cities, are full of people who do not observe the laws of Islam, and so crime can still be found – but if the authorities carry out punishments, it is a strong deterrent.

——— Cutting the hand for theft ———

Let us take an example. Cutting off the hand is the Islamic punishment for theft; but the Middle East is not crammed full of one-handed people. In true Islamic company, the very idea of theft is unthinkable, the biggest deterrent being the knowledge that Allah can see everything you do and if you committed theft it would be recorded against you in your book, for the Day of Judgement. The second big deterrent is the shame that knowledge of your theft would bring not only on your family but on your whole village (if you lived in a small community).

Local laws might be rough and ready, but under Islam the amputation of the hand should not be meted out casually, an accused person being dragged off to a block and summarily punished. The case should be examined carefully, and there have to be witnesses. If it can be proved that the reason the person stole was in some way the inadequacy of the state or local ruler or community (say, for example, that someone stole food for their family because they could not find work to pay for it), then the thief should not be held at fault, but the community, and work and money should be found for the thief and his family.

If, however, it was a case of someone being addicted to picking up other people's property without any qualms or conscience about it, then Shariat law would not hesitate to order amputation.

'If your hand causes you to sin, cut it off. It is better for you to enter life maimed than with two hands to go to Hell.' (Mark 9:43)

This is intended to stop the person from sinning any further, as well as warning the community that they have a thief in their midst, and giving the deliberately callous thief just punishment for the hurt he or she has caused. Some scholars think that the best way to 'cut off the hand of the thief' is to create a society in which theft is unnecessary. In an ideal society, with all citizens and laws truly Muslim, this would be the case.

The Prophet commented that he would carry out this punishment against a deliberate thief, no matter how highly placed and influential, even if it were his own daughter Fatimah!

—— Flogging for drunkenness ——

Following the same kind of principles, Shariat law also administers flogging for drunkenness. This seems particularly harsh to societies in the west that have grown accustomed to most adults consuming alcohol. In Islamic society there is no drinking of alcohol, but, again, the main deterrent is the knowledge that Allah knows everything that you do, and not the fear of savage punishment.

The effects of alcohol on society are very well known, as are the figures for associated criminal activity; everything from drunken driving to public disorder and causing public nuisance, from wife-beating to burning the house down accidentally, to lessened responsibility with its attendant ill-mannered and loutish conduct.

In the time of the Prophet there was a great deal of similar consumption of alcohol, but the revelation of the Qur'an forbade it. Even then, the Prophet did not consider it right deliberately to seek out and hound people who consumed alcohol in the privacy of their own homes; that was their business. If people are flogged for having alcohol in their homes, they are the 'victims' of the law of the land and not Islamic law. But he did not hesitate to flog those who were drunk and abusive on the streets. It is not known whether any abused wives complained to him for justice against their husbands, but he would undoubtedly have given it.

Incidentally, there are numerous rules governing the administration of Islamic flogging; it is not just a savage beating inflicted capriciously according to the whims of brutal guards. It has to be done with control, in accord with justice, and in the kindest possible way in the circumstances, following a long list of stipulations, including deferment when someone is sick, not to touch face, head or private parts, women to be fully clothed and allowed to sit, not to be done on days of extreme heat or cold, and so forth.

—— Execution for adultery ——

As regards adultery, women's honour is highly regarded in Islam, and the woman of any age has the right to be treated according to her position; as a protected virgin, a respected wife and partner, an honoured mother or grandmother. If a marriage breaks down, then divorce is allowed, and Islam does not require people to struggle to live on in unhappy relationships. Adultery is considered as the theft of a husband or wife, a theft of the most serious nature; any partner who gave in to such temptation willingly would be despised.

However, the Prophet knew from personal experience the trauma of having his beloved wife accused of adultery, and the seed of suspicion planted in his own mind. Allah gave him specific personal revelation as a result of this case: the death penalty only applied to committed, married, free Muslim citizens; no person was to be found guilty and executed for adultery unless it was committed in public and witnessed by four witnesses; anyone who gave false witness, or made slanderous accusations without proof, should himself or herself be flogged.

In some countries, however, the law of the land allows guilty adulterers to be stoned to death, and in Saudi Arabia they could be beheaded. However, for a true Muslim, there should be no sexual activity outside marriage. (See divorce, pages 183-185)

Islamic motives

The justice of Allah is not to see wrongdoers relentlessly hunted down and made to suffer retribution, but the powerful desire to see peace, right and order restored, by the removal of the failing, weakness or enmity that lay behind the wrong. If someone has been wronged, it is the duty of all Muslims to unite to have the wrong put right. Muslims can never think it right to turn a blind eye to injustice, or let it go unchallenged. That is seen as weakness, and counter to the will of God.

Allah is always merciful, and He may indeed forgive you if you are sorry; but if you have wronged another person, then their demands of justice have to be fulfilled. God always counsels a merciful attitude:

'The reward for an injury is an equal injury back; but if a person forgives instead and is reconciled, that will earn reward from Allah.' (Surah 42:40)

However, if refusal to take action over the wrong is really because of weakness, laziness or fear, then the so-called 'forgiveness' is not genuine at all, but only a cheap alternative to the action of seeking to put right. The resentment is still there, the wound still festering.

God's justice

Finally, every Muslim believes that human judgements can be wrong, or influenced by bias or ignorance of the circumstances, but Allah sees and hears everything, and no person can escape their true judgement on their life. The Prophet knew the frailty of human judgement and warned his followers that if anyone knowingly allowed judgement to be given against someone they had accused wrongly, they would pay for it before the justice of Allah:

> *'When you bring your case to me, some of you may be more eloquent in expressing their side than others. I will judge based upon what I hear, and if I happen to give someone something belonging to his fellow citizen, he should not take it, for I would be giving him a piece of the fire!' (Hadith Bukhari, Malik, Ahmad)*

On that Day, no one will be able to make excuses for another – we will all stand alone, as individuals, with the true record of our lives.

17

– WORK AND WEALTH –

The economic principles of Islam are to build up a just society in which people behave responsibly and honestly, and are enabled to find honourable employment that is not exploitative, corrupt, or based on cheating and swindling.

Earning for the family is still the responsibility of the Muslim man in most Islamic societies, although there is no ruling in Islam to prevent women from going out to honourable work.

———— The importance of work ————

It is considered very important that a person does work, and does not stay idle or become a burden to others. It is considered very dishonourable to be a parasite on society, unless, of course, one is unable to work through illness or other handicap. Begging is strongly disapproved of, unless there is no other alternative and it is a case of extreme necessity.

'Receiving charity is permissible for three sorts of people only; one who is in grinding poverty, one who is seriously in debt, or one who is responsible for a debt and finds it difficult to pay.' (Abu Dawud)

Even people who have to be supported by others because of their devotion to religion are disapproved of:

'Some people once came to the Prophet (pbuh) in the company of a hermit – a religious recluse. The Prophet (pbuh) said: "Who is he?" They said: "He is a man who has devoted himself to worship." The

Prophet (pbuh) then said: "Who feeds him?" They said: "We all do."
He said: "Then all of you are better than he is."' (Bukhari and
Muslim)

On the other hand, any work one does for anybody else (providing it
is acceptable in Islam) is counted as if it was done for Allah:

'The Prophet's companions once noticed a man's fortitude and
perseverance at work and said: "O Messenger – this man would be
really wonderful if only his actions were for the cause of Allah." The
Prophet (pbuh) said: "If he goes to work to support his young children,
his old parents, or even for the satisfaction of his own needs, then
all his work is regarded as a jihad in the cause of Allah. But if he
goes to work in order to boast and be proud, it is in the cause of the
Devil."' (Bukhari)

—— Lawful and unlawful work ——

Islam makes a difference between lawful and unlawful methods of earning a living.

'No body which has been nourished with what is unlawful shall enter
Paradise.' (Ahmad, Darmi and Baihaqi)

Basically, if someone's means of earning a living hurts another, or
results in another's loss, it is haram (forbidden). If it is fair and beneficial, then it is halal (allowed). Obviously, any form of making money
that involves dishonesty, deceit or fraud, bribery, robbery, hoarding in
order to take advantage of hardship, exploitation, artificial creation of
shortages, or anything to do with alcohol, gambling or lotteries, sexual
degradation or immoral practices, is forbidden to Muslims.

The Prophet made it very clear that people who made a living against
the spirit of Islam would gain no benefit from their practice of religion
– their bad livelihood would cancel out the benefits of their visits to the
mosque!

'People make long prayers to Allah although their food and their
clothes are unlawfully acquired. How can the prayer of such people be
accepted?' (Muslim and Tirmidhi)

— The dignity of the menial worker —

The Prophet taught that there was no room in Islam for snobbery. There was no disgrace or humiliation in doing menial work, or work that was 'looked down on' by those better off. The only shame was in depending on others for hand-outs when you were capable of helping yourself. Communities need rubbish collectors just as much as professors. Nobody need regard any useful employment as being beneath them, and Islam gave dignity to many professions previously considered lowly and degrading. The office cleaner has as much dignity and worth in the eyes of Allah as the manager of a business empire. What counts is his or her dignity, honesty, and attitude towards the work he or she is doing.

— Collective responsibilities —

Muslim economy regards certain crafts and industries as essential to the community, those known as *fard kifiyah* or 'collective obligations'. Every Muslim community should try to include people to meet the needs of education, medicine, science and technology, politics and community welfare, and clothing, utensil and agricultural industries. All productive resources should be brought into use as far as possible, and not left idle or wasted, including unemployed manpower, unused land, and water or mineral resources.

— The duty of employees —

Employed people have a duty to their employers, as well as to those they support, so they should not cheat on hours for which payment is claimed, or be lazy, or encourage any practice in the workplace which cheats the employer in some way.

They should not waste money irresponsibly, or fritter it away on worthless and wasteful things. Extravagance and waste are strongly discouraged in Islam.

The duties of employers towards
———————— employees ————————

Employers should treat their employees with justice and kindness, and should pay them fairly, without undue delay.

'Give the worker his wages before his sweat dries.' (Ibn Majah)

Workers should be protected adequately from danger in the workplace, and not exploited or made to work unreasonable hours, or worked to exhaustion in appalling conditions, with no opportunity to take rest or refreshment.

'An employer should not ask an employee to do anything beyond his capacity. If that which the master demands is necessary, the master himself should lend a helping hand to the servant.' (Bukhari)

— Making interest on money – Riba —

Making interest on loaned money (known as *riba*) is regarded as a despicable capitalising on another person's misfortune or need, and is totally forbidden by the Qur'an. Charging interest makes rich people richer and the poor poorer, since they are forced into more debt and dependency. This is why Muslim societies establish their own Islamic Banks, which have worked out honourable ways of utilising deposited money without the system of giving or taking interest on money, according to the complicated Shariat laws.

'Allah has permitted trade but forbidden usury; those who cease the practice after hearing our Lord's command will be pardoned for their past sins . . . but those who repeat the offence will be companions of the fire.' (Surah 2:278)

'Cursed be the one who accepts usury, the one who paid it, the witness to it, and the one who recorded it.' (Abu Dawud)

Riba means any unjustified advantage in trade dealings, and has a wider meaning than the simple notion of taking 'interest' on one's money in the bank. In Islam, in order to be honourable, money has to be used as a facility and not a commodity, or the owners of money gain an unfair advantage over the producers or traders. They could wait until the merchandise lost value (as in food crops and other perishables) and force merchants to sell at a low price; or they could buy up commodities and hoard them until they increase in value. These practices are forbidden in Islam; wealth should be in circulation and not hoarded away for the private benefit of a few. To regulate this, Islamic governments impose a tax on all money which is not spent in circulation, and providers of funds can only share the profits provided they are also willing to share the losses.

18

SEX

Sex is regarded in Islam as the gift of Allah that gives the human being, in a small way, the experience of the bliss of Paradise, in advance. It is a basic and fundamental urge in human beings, and in the search for sexual fulfilment people can give each other great joy and happiness, but it can also give enormous scope for great despair and hurt.

Celibacy

Since sex is a creation and gift of Allah, Muslims cannot regard it as evil and unclean, or that it should be resisted and suppressed. People who choose to be celibate for religious reasons are not approved of in Islam; that would be seen to be a form of ingratitude towards Allah which might lead to a dangerously stressed, repressed or perverted personality.

> *'Sa'id b. Abu Waqqas recorded that when Uthman b. Mazun decided to live in celibacy, Allah's Messenger (pbuh) forbade him to do so.'*
> *(Muslim)*

On the other hand, the gratification of sexual urges without moral considerations is also regarded as an abuse of Allah's intention; Islam seeks for sexual desires to be satisfied, but that the individual and the family are protected from dangerous consequences.

—— The dangers of sexual freedom ——

Not only does Islam prohibit sexual activity before marriage, it does not condone any kind of privacy between unrelated people of the opposite sex past the age of puberty who are not married to each other, in order to avoid temptation.

> *'Let no man be in privacy with a woman who is not lawful to him, or Satan will be the third.' (Tirmidhi)*

The Prophet knew that it was natural for men to see a woman and be stirred physically; that is why Allah requested that men and women should not seek to be alone together, that they should not tempt each other by seductive clothing or ways or looks; and that if a man happened to feel a sexual urge for someone other than his wife while out, he should

> *'go straight to his wife and have intercourse with her, for that would repel what he had felt.' (Muslim, Abu Dawud)*

—————— Homosexuality ——————

> *'Of all the creatures in the world, will you approach males and abandon those whom God created for you as mates?' (Surah 26:165)*

The Qur'an not only forbids homosexuality, but the Prophet also declared that women should not wear male clothing and vice versa; neither should imitate the opposite sex in their ways of speaking, walking or moving.

—————— Sex within marriage ——————

The Prophet said:

> *'Having sexual intercourse with one's wife is* sadaqah *(loving charity).' (Abu Dawud)*

He also said:

> 'When a husband and wife share intimacy it is rewarded, and a blessing from Allah; just as it would be punished if they had indulged in illicit sex.' (Muslim)

When people read the hadith, they are often surprised to discover that the Prophet was not in the least prudish. He frequently answered questions of a most basic and intimate nature, and gave advice to people with a whole range of highly personal problems – everything from menstruation to sexual impotency. His advice was always very kind and down to earth, and based on the desire to serve Allah in every facet of life, including the satisfaction one could give to one's marital partner.

Since no Muslim is allowed to have sex with anyone other than their marriage partner, both partners have a duty to love, honour and satisfy the needs of their spouses. If either side neglects this duty, it is bound to cause suffering, depression, and lead to the breakdown of the relationship.

The Prophet was very concerned about male selfishness, which was commonplace in his society. He urged his male followers many times to take care of and respect their wives, and cherish them. With regard to sexual intimacy, they were to turn their activity into sadaqah (charity) by not flinging themselves upon their women as if they were no more than animals, or just satisfying their own urges and then leaving their women disappointed and frustrated.

> 'A muslim man should not satisfy his need of her until he has satisfied her need of him.' (al-Ghassali)

Women were expected to be compliant to their husbands' wishes, and to fulfil their needs. If wives or husbands refused each other, the Prophet said that 'the angels would curse them until morning'.

> 'By Him in Whose hand is my life, when a man calls his wife to his bed and she does not respond, the One in Heaven is displeased with her until her husband is pleased with her.' (Muslim)

In an Islamic marriage, neither partner should try to force the other one to do anything which is distasteful or unpleasant or painful to them. Marital rape should never take place, or abuse of the wife.

Discretion

The Prophet requested that marital relationships should be discreet, and intimate details not divulged to any outsiders which would be hurtful and embarrassing to the partner concerned.

> *'The most wicked of people is the man who goes to his wife, and she comes to him, and he then divulges her secret.' (Muslim, Abu Dawud)*

Sexual education

Muslims do not feel that instruction from strangers (whose own personal morals they do not know) is a good thing, hence there is much resistance to sexual education programmes in schools.

However, wives and husbands have a duty to make their marriage as happy as possible, and, therefore, although Muslim youngsters are not exposed to the sexual experimentation now common in the West, it is their duty to know how to please their partners, and to strive to do this with the same Islamic dedication that they strive to do their best for Allah in any other sphere of life.

19

— WOMEN'S RIGHTS —

Every instruction given to Muslims in the Qur'an refers to both male and female believers alike. They have been given the same religious duties and will be judged according to exactly the same criteria.

> *'For Muslim men and women, for believing men and women . . .*
> *for men and women who are patient and constant, who humble*
> *themselves, who give in charity, who fast, who guard their chastity,*
> *who engage in the praise of Allah – for them Allah has prepared*
> *forgiveness and a great reward.' (Surah 33:35)*

This particular verse was the answer from Allah given in direct response to the Prophet's wife Umm Salamah, who asked him one day why the Qur'an revelations never specifically mentioned women.

Muslim doctrine holds that women are not in any way inferior beings to men, but were created originally from the same single soul (see Surah 4:1). Muslim women are granted equal rights in Islam as well as equal responsibilities.

Muslim women do not regard domestic life in the home as being in any way subservient, but of vital importance to the well-being of the family, and they are encouraged just as much as men to become educated and useful members of the community. To seek knowledge is the duty of *every* Muslim.

—————— Male supremacy ——————

Islam gives men 'supremacy' over women only in certain very limited aspects. They have a 'degree of advantage over them' (Surah 2:228) when it comes to running the home, or in initiating divorce proceedings.

This was because in general men were the providers of the family finances, responsible for caring for their women and child.

Divorce settlements and inheritance laws in Islamic countries also bear in mind the financial responsibilities of the men. However, the laws of Islam were revolutionary in their insistence on the rights of females, even those of female orphans (who were previously regarded virtually as property and callously manoeuvred in marriage in order to gain their money).

Women and work

There is no Islamic injunction against women going out to work, so long as that work is compatible with Islamic principles, and does not threaten the security and well-being of the home. Muslim women are just as entitled as non-Muslims to employ household staff so that they can take other employment themselves – but many Muslim women do not wish to do this, or to leave the raising of their children to others.

Muslim women have the right to be provided for, and their men should not force them to go out to earn money. However, there is no text that prevents a woman from seeking work if she so wishes, provided it is an occupation acceptable in Islam. The Prophet's first wife, Khadijah, was a highly successful business woman, who was the Prophet's employer before she became his wife.

Even if the woman happens to be more wealthy than her husband, he has the duty to keep her, and should not rely on her for support.

Seclusion of women

Purdah, or seclusion of women, was a practice used extensively by upper class Hindus, Persians, Byzantines and even some Christians, who did not allow their women equality. It has nothing to do with Islam, but is a cultural matter, although these days it is largely Muslim societies where the practice persists.

Purdah implies complete segregation of men from women, and in many

Muslim societies the women have a separate and private part of the house (or even tent), and may use separate entrances. Most mosques have separate entrances for men and women, because the women pray at the back, but they usually rejoin their menfolk afterwards.

Muslim women are not required to be hidden away at all times, although in many cultures Muslim women are very shy of strangers. In the Prophet's day, women went regularly to the mosque to pray with the men, despite the attempts of many of those men to keep them away. The Prophet's wife Aisha reported:

> *'I used to set out towards the mosque and observe prayer along with Allah's Messenger (pbuh); and I was in the row of women nearest the row of men.' (Muslim)*

In today's world, you will see Muslim women in public in every country and culture, and they will all be modestly dressed.

Wearing a full-covering veil while in public is a kind of halfway purdah. Where Muslim women are reluctant to talk to strangers, wearing a chador gives complete privacy and anonymity. People do not disturb, talk to, bother, or flirt with ladies in purdah. The black veils are taken off once the women are safely inside again.

In some parts of the world women hide their faces from strangers and yet are not Muslim; and elsewhere devout Muslim women do not veil because this would be regarded as odd, or attention-seeking.

The less extreme Muslim hijab allows women to go about freely, but protected from the lures of the world by modest dress.

Extremist seclusion was not the Prophet's sunnah, and may have arisen from a narrow interpretation of the following verses addressed specifically to the Prophet's wives:

> *'O wives of the Prophet! You are not like ordinary women. If you fear Allah, don't be too casual in your speech, lest someone with an unsteadfast heart should be moved with desire . . . live quietly in your houses, and don't make a worldly display as in the times of ignorance; establish regular prayer and give regular charity, and obey Allah and His Apostle.' (Surah 33:32–33)*

True Islamic motives

A woman's standards of behaviour and dress should never be from pressure of others, but simply because she herself has the desire to please Allah, and submit to Him, even in the matter of her clothing. In fact, in certain societies, some Muslim women have taken to wearing hijab in spite of opposition from their husbands, or secular governments.

Purdah

However, many Muslim men from the Asian subcontinent, and from various Arab countries, will not allow their womenfolk to mix with males outside the family circle; this practice is declining as, all over the world, Muslim women are receiving education and taking up employment.

Exploitation of women

The Prophet was alert to unfortunate women being exploited in work situations, and commented on the injustices done to women workers in this way:

> '*Allah will definitely enforce the settlement of the dues of those entitled to receive them on the Day of Judgement; even the wrong done to the hornless goat (i.e. the female) by the horned goat (i.e. the male) will be redressed!*' (*Muslim*)

Any woman working to increase the financial income of her family should have the same rights as a male worker, and should not be taken advantage of, or subjected to any form of harassment (especially not sexual harassment). Wearing hijab when in public places (including the workplace) helps to discourage amorous male advances.

She also has the right to fair wages, and decent conditions of work. If a so-called Muslim employer is using women more or less as slave-labour, it is an abuse and he or she is flying in the face of Islamic principles and will ultimately be called to account for it.

The right to be protected

Islam takes note of the physical differences between the sexes; it does not assume that men and women are 'the same'. Thoughtful allowances should be made to protect woman and make them comfortable. Men do not have to endure menstruation, pregnancy, childbirth and suckling children. Men are not usually harassed because of their attractiveness, or forced to accept sex in order to 'get on', or not lose a job.

A Muslim woman has the right to be cared for at times of physical pain and discomfort.

> *'Men are the protectors and maintainers of women, because God has given them more strength . . . therefore righteous women are devoutly obedient, and guard in the husband's absence that which God would have them guard.' (Surah 4:34)*

Muslim women usually cover their heads with some kind of scarf or veil, and cover their arms and legs, according to the request of the Prophet.

> *'"O Asma," (said the Prophet to his wife's younger sister), "when a girl reaches puberty it is not proper that anything of her should remain exposed except this and this," and he pointed to her face and the palms of her hands.' (Abu Dawud)*

Culture problems

In many cultures women have been and still are subjected to all sorts of abuses from their chauvinistic menfolk; sometimes these cultures have taken up Islam as their religion, but the full principles of Islam have not yet overcome the cultural male chauvinism. It is hardly fair, in these circumstances, to blame Islam for the suppression of women, when Allah (through the Qur'an) and the Prophet tried so hard to convince men that misuse and abuse of women was wrong.

20

DRUGS, ALCOHOL ── AND TOBACCO ──

Any substance which intoxicates is known in Arabic as *khamr*, and is forbidden to Muslims.

> '*Allah has cursed khamr, those who produce it, those for whom it is produced, those who drink it, those who serve it, those who carry it, those it is carried to, those who sell it and those who buy it.*'
> *(Tirmidhi)*

Muslims cannot enter the state of wudu if they are not in full possession of their senses, or have drug- or alcohol-clouded minds; the word 'khamara' means 'veiled, covered or concealed'.

> '*Every intoxicant is khamr, and every intoxicant is forbidden.*'
> *(Muslim)*

─── Alcohol ───

At the time of the Prophet, alcohol was consumed in large quantities, and the antisocial effects of drunkenness were very well known. Allah's prohibition, interestingly enough, took human weakness into account, and was given in stages over quite a long period of time.

First, it was pointed out that good and evil could come from the same object; both nourishing and harmful products can actually come from the same plant – the date vine:

> *'And from the fruit of the date-palm and the vine you can derive wholesome fruit and drink. Behold, there is a sign in this for the wise.' (Surah 16:67)*

The second revelation pointed out that the harm of khamr far outweighed the good, but it was still not forbidden. People were left to form their own judgements:

> *'When they ask you concerning wine and gambling, say: In them is great sin and a little profit; but the sin is greater than the profit.' (Surah 2:218)*

Next came the request that Muslims should not be intoxicated when they come to prayer:

> *'O believers! Do not come to prayer with a befogged mind, but come when you can fully understand all that you are saying.' (Surah 4:43)*

Finally came the order, the complete prohibition:

> *'O believers! Intoxicants, gambling and trying to foretell the future are the lures of Satan; if you wish to prosper, you must keep away from these things. It is Satan's plan to stir up enmity and hatred in your midst with them, and lure you away from remembering Allah.' (Surah 93–94)*

(If you look at the references, you will see that the verses do not come in chronological order in the Qur'an, but are given in the actual order they were received by the Prophet before the order of the Qur'an was also revealed towards the end of his life.)

The effect of the prohibition

As news of the revelation spread like wildfire, the Muslims poured away any alcohol they were drinking and got rid of their stores; no 100 per cent Muslim has touched alcohol ever since.

Obviously, one can find plenty of weak Muslims who do drink. Some argue that drinking in moderation is not harmful. This is not acceptable, really, because it breaks the command of Allah.

> *'If a bucketful intoxicates, a sip of it is haram.' (Ahmad, Abu Dawud, Tirmidhi)*

There is no penalty laid down in the Qur'an for drinking, but a flogging was the mildest punishment laid down for slander and abuse, and as the consumption of alcohol often makes people abusive and slanderous, flogging is sometimes ordered for publicly offensive drunk behaviour. It is not part of Shariat law to pry into private dwellings or secretly spy on people to catch them out, but any antisocial, threatening or dangerous behaviour caused by alcohol that is witnessed is always dealt with.

Has the Muslim who drinks left Islam? Those who believe in Islamic principles would probably reply that just as one cannot continue to commit theft or other crimes and still regard oneself as a believer, the same must apply to alcohol-taking by analogy.

Alcohol in medicine

The Prophet disapproved of the use of alcohol in medicine, even when it formed the base or preservative in the medicine:

Alcohol is not a medicine but a disease.' (Muslim, Tirmidhi)

'Allah has sent down the disease and the cure, and for every disease there is a cure. So take medicine; but do not use anything haram as a medicine.' (Abu Dawud)

Muslims should consult the pharmacist before taking medicine, and if offered one with alcohol, should enquire whether an alternative was available. If there was no alternative, the alcohol base would be allowed, as, in cases of dire necessity, that which is haram may become halal.

——————————— Drugs ———————————

The plant world is full of substances which affect the human body and mind, and nowadays the medical profession manufactures artificial substances also, to give similar effects. Their use to provide cures for illness is not forbidden in Islam.

However, many drugs, such as marijuana, cocaine, opium, nicotine, etc – powerful intoxicants which affect the human mind – are also classed as khamr. They are frequently misused in a harmful way, totally in opposition to the spirit of Islam.

'Sinful people smoke hashish because they find it produces rapture and delight, an effect similar to drunkenness . . . it promotes dullness and lethargy . . . it disturbs the mind and temperament, excites sexual desire, and leads to shameless promiscuity.' (Sheikh ibn Taymiyyah)

Drugs are used to escape from the pains and distresses of life, or to indulge in exciting fantasy experience and artificially induced euphoria. Those who start off as experimenters could soon find themselves on the downward spiral to crime, physical decline, and moral insensitivity.

The Muslim general principle against drugs misuse is the same as that for alcohol, based on the acceptance that Allah owns our bodies, and anything which harms or injures them is haram.

Smoking

Smoking has not been declared haram in Islam, and millions of Muslims smoke. However, it is obvious that if one extends the principles of not doing harm to oneself or others, then smoking can never be an approved exercise. Non-smokers have the right to breathe clean air, unpolluted by others. Muslims, if they must smoke, should do so with discretion and not damage other people's furnishings, or set a bad example to the young, or encourage those who have given up to start again.

21

FRIENDSHIP
AND UNITY

The worldwide community of Muslims is known as the Ummah. It extends across all places and ethnic groupings. Believers belong to local ummahs, or Muslim communities, but the entire worldwide Muslim community follows the same faith, shares the same basic values, and has sworn allegiance to the will of Allah and obedience to the Prophet. When they travel around the world, they find they can mix very easily with other Muslims, even if they do not understand their language.

Things like praying in Arabic and facing the qibla of Makkah also help to kindle the spirit of unity throughout the Muslims of the world. Muslims can never forget that the faith of Islam is a universal faith, intended for all people.

No race of people should ever consider itself better than any other; all people are equal, irrespective of faith, language, race, belief and so forth.

The Prophet was told by Allah as part of His revelation to say:

'O humanity! I am the messenger of God to you all!' (Surah 7:158)

──────── Muslim unity ────────

The unity of believers was one of the Prophet's top priorities; one's 'brothers' were no longer just members of one's own family, but all believers in the 'family' of Islam. Each individual was part of the whole, each person important and cherished. Believers were to love each other, and support each other, and take care of each other in times of need.

'If any single part of the body aches, the whole body feels the effects of it and rushes to its relief.' (Muslim)

'Believers are like parts of a building; each part supports the others.' (Muslim)

Non-Muslims often cannot understand why Muslims in one part of the world get so worked up over what they regard as injustices done to Muslims in other parts of the world; they do not understand the deep feelings of ummah Muslims have for each other, or the duty of support they feel towards each other.

──────── Muslim division ────────

Unfortunately, it is also obvious that the family of Islam suffers from splits, rivalries, jealousies, and nationalism. Far too many issues divide the Muslims of different countries and cultures, which is not the fault of Islam, simply of the incomplete or inaccurate understanding of it. While the Prophet was still alive, he regretted the divisive instinct that spoiled the peace of his own community of believers.

Allah Himself stated:

'Believers are one single brotherhood, so make peace and reconciliation between two contenders, and fear Allah, that you may receive mercy.' (Surah 49:10)

The Prophet commented:

'The devil is a wolf to humanity, catching the one which is solitary, the one who strays from the flock, and the one which wanders. So

avoid the branching paths, and keep to the general community!'
(Ahmad)

The Prophet hated sectarianism and exclusivism; he disapproved of
extremists pushing themselves forward and causing rivalry and hurt
feelings and enmity. However, although it is patently obvious that many
Muslims fall far short of the ideal, nevertheless the ideal of the Ummah
is there to be aimed at.

Friendship

Muslims are not supposed to abstain from the world in order to find
'religious purity'. They are part of the world, and must live out their
faith in their communities. The Prophet set the example, living in
the midst of his followers and showing them how to live by his
personal example. Islam disapproves of monasticism, and encourages
people to mix and cooperate. Friendships are a vital part of life, and
highly influential in moulding the individual's mind and attitude.
Muslims, therefore, consider it very important to choose their friends
wisely.

*'A person is apt to follow the faith of his friend, so be careful with
whom you make friends.' (Ahmad and Abu Dawud)*

Those to avoid

If friendship is based on love of Allah and commitment to the faith,
Muslims believe it will be blessed. On the other hand, they are warned
against becoming too friendly with people who may try to influence
them away from Islam.

*'On that day, the wrongdoer will bite at his hands and say: "O would
that I had taken the straight path! Woe is me! Would that I had
never taken such a one for a friend. He led me astray."' (Surah
25:27–30)*

Muslims are very serious about their religion, so they usually avoid
people who take faith as a joke, belittle it, or deliberately agitate against
it.

'Leave alone those who take religion to be mere play and amusement, and are deceived by the life of this world; proclaim to them this truth – that every soul delivers itself to ruin by its own acts.' (Surah 6:70)

Good friendship

Having a good friend is a wonderful gift of God, and a treasure worth protecting. Muslims should make a deliberate effort to be good and loyal friends, who are worth having. Good friendship is always unselfish and considerate. Muslims are encouraged to keep in close touch with their friends, not neglecting them for more than a few days, and to be aware of their needs and distresses.

Muslims are also expected to avoid gossip and backbiting, hurtful jokes, embarrassing remarks, snobbery, or fault-finding.

'Beware of suspicion, for suspicion is a great falsehood. Do not search for faults in each other, do not spy on each other, nor yearn after that which others possess, nor envy, nor entertain malice nor indifference; do not turn away from one another, and be servants of Allah, but brothers to one another as you have been ordered.' (Muslim, Malik)

If people practise sympathy, tolerance, unselfishness and genuine concern for each other, they will be actively carrying out the will of God.

'Don't sever ties of kinship, don't bear enmity against one another, don't nurse aversion for one another, and don't feel envy against the other. Live as fellow brothers, as Allah has commanded you.' (Muslim)

22

—— GREEN ISLAM ——

'The whole Earth has been created a place of worship, pure and clean.' (Muslim)

To be 'green' means to care for the environment, the world in which we live, both on the intimate and local level, and in the wider sense of caring for the well-being of the planet.

Both aims are specifically a part of Islam, for God required his created humans to be His *khalifas* (rulers for Him), in looking after the planet and using it in the best possible way.

'It is He who has made you custodians, inheritors of the Earth.' (Surah 6:165)

After many centuries of neglect and exploitation by people who simply saw the planet's resources as a free gift to be exploited so that they could get rich quick, it has now become fashionable to be green, and to worry about what has happened.

Muslims are required to care for the planet, and not to waste, damage, pollute or destroy it. On the Day of Judgement, they will be asked about their responsibility towards the Earth and its creatures.

—————— Green individuals ——————

Muslims can follow green principles in all sorts of ways, mainly by being aware of what they are doing, and by avoiding waste and pollution. Everyday products should be used and recycled as much as possible, energy use should be cut down, products such as fur or ivory, obtained from the killing of rare or endangered species of animals should not be bought, nor should those that have been tested on animals captured or bred for this purpose.

Muslims should use biodegradable products as far as possible, prefer unleaded petrol and detergents that do not pollute the water supply.

> *'Whoever plants a tree and diligently looks after it until it matures and bears fruit, Allah will count as charity for him anything for which its fruits are used.' (Ahmad)*

───────── Animals ─────────

Since Allah loves every creature He has made, the principles of mercy and compassion should be extended to every living creature.

> *'All creatures are Allah's children, and those dearest to Allah are those who treat His children kindly.' (Baihaqi)*

It is forbidden for Muslims to be cruel or even inconsiderate to the animals that live and work among them. All domestic animals (whether pets or farm livestock) should be properly fed, housed and looked after.

Beasts of burden should not be made to carry or pull loads too heavy for them, or to labour until they are exhausted, or their flesh has raw patches and sores – a common enough sight in many so-called Islamic societies where true Islam is not being carried out.

───────── Hunting ─────────

Islam rejects hunting and killing just for sport and amusement; one may take the life of animals only for food or other genuinely useful purpose.

> *'If someone kills (even) a sparrow for sport, the sparrow will cry out on the Day of Judgement: "O Lord! That person killed me for nothing! He did not kill me for any useful purpose!"' (al-Nisai, Ibn Hibban)*

Where animals have a natural hunting instinct (such as hawks or dogs) they cannot be blamed for doing what comes naturally to them – but deliberate cruelty is never encouraged. Animals used for hunting should be well trained, under control, and not clumsy or savage.

If animals are hunted with weapons, they must not be blunt (like clubs for bludgeoning), but efficient and able to pierce the animal (such as spear, sword or bullet) and not such as would club it or throttle it.

Blood-sports

Any sport which involves goading one animal to fight another is forbidden in Islam. This includes dog fights and cock-fights. All sports involving hunting down and killing animals for fun are also forbidden, such as fox-hunting, badger, bear or dog baiting, and bullfighting.

The luxury trade

Any destruction of animal life simply to satisfy the vanity of wealthy ladies is abhorrent to Islam. No Muslim could condone the clubbing of baby seals, for example, or hunting beautiful animals to extinction for their fur, or horn, or tusks.

However, the Prophet did not approve of waste, and if an animal died or was killed for food, Muslims were encouraged to use its skin, horns, bones, hair or hide.

—————— Factory farming ——————

Unnatural or cruel methods of farming which deprive livestock of all enjoyment of life are forbidden in Islam, such as keeping them in cramped and dark conditions, force-feeding them unnatural foodstuffs in order to interfere with their natural flavour or fat content, and making them grow unnaturally quickly so that their natural life is unreasonably shortened.

Slaughter

Animal slaughter should always be by the halal method, which Muslims maintain is the kindest possible way. It should be done with a very sharp knife, and in an atmosphere that does not cause the animal panic or distress. Animals should not be killed in front of each other.

> *Ibn Abbas once recorded that the Prophet saw a man who was sharpening his knife after laying down a sheep to be slaughtered. He rebuked him saying: 'Do you intend to make it die two deaths? Why did you not sharpen your knife before lying it down?' (al-Hakim)*

It is forbidden to deny food or drink to an animal on the grounds that it is just about to be killed.

Animal experiments and vivisection

Any experimentation solely for reasons of luxury goods and vanity is forbidden in Islam. Muslims should enquire carefully whether the products they buy have been produced by halal methods – those which do not inflict suffering or cruelty.

23

—— ISLAMIC ETHICS ——

*'God does not look upon your bodies and appearances; He looks upon
your hearts and deeds.' (Baihaqi)*

The aim of Islam is to promote certain values specifically, and deliberately try to reduce or stamp out others.

The key values in Islam are:

Faith

*'You should worship God as if you are seeing Him, for He sees you
even if you do not see Him.' (Muslim)*

Justice

*'O believers, be seekers after justice, witnesses for God, even though
it be against yourselves or your parents and kinsmen.' (Surah 4:133)*

Forgiveness

*'Be forgiving and control yourself in the face of provocation; give
justice to the person who was unfair and unjust to you; give to
someone even though he did not give to you when you were in need,
and keep fellowship with the one who did not reciprocate your
concern.' (Bukhari)*

Compassion

*'He who has no compassion for our little ones . . . is not one of us.'
(Muslim)*

Mercy

'Hold tight to the rope of God, and never let it go. Remember that

God showed mercy to you and blessed you while you were still enemies. Remember how He united your hearts together in love, so that by His grace you became brothers.' (Surah 3:103)

Sincerity

'God does not accept belief if it is not expressed in deeds; and He does not accept your deeds unless they conform to your beliefs.' (Muslim)

Truth

'Always speak the truth, even if it is bitter.' (Baihaqi)

Generosity

'The truly virtuous person . . . gives food, for the love of Him, to the needy, the orphan, the captive, (saying): "We feed you only for the sake of Allah; we desire no recompense from you and no thanks."' (Surah 76:7–10)

'An ignorant man who is generous is dearer to God than a worshipper who is miserly.' (Tirmidhi)

Humility

'The one who is humble for the sake of Allah will be exalted by Allah, for though he considers himself lowly he is great in the eyes of men; but he who is proud will be abased by Allah, for though he considers himself great he is lowly in the eyes of men to such an extent that he is of less value than a dog or a pig.' (Baihaqi)

Tolerance

'Let there be no coercion in religion.' (Surah 2:256)

Modesty

'Modesty and faith are joined closely together; if either of them is lost, the other goes also.' (Muslim, Baihaqi)

Chastity

'The fornicator who fornicates is not a believer so long as he commits it.' (Ahmad)

Patience and fortitude

'Muslims who live in the midst of society and bear with patience the afflictions that come to them are better than those who shun society and cannot bear any wrong done to them.' (Abu Dawud)

Responsibility

'Every one of you is a shepherd, and will be questioned about the well-being of his flock.' (Muslim)

Courage

'Fight in the cause of Allah those who fight you, but do not go beyond the limits . . . for tyranny and oppression are worse than murder.' (Surah 2:190)

The key things which are abhorred are:

Hypocrisy

'Woe to those who pray but are unmindful of their prayer, or pray only to be seen by people.' (Surah 107:6–7)

Cheating

'The truthful and trusty merchant is associated with the prophets, the upright and the martyrs.' (Tirmidhi, Darimi)

Backbiting and suspicion

'O believers, avoid suspicion, for suspicion is a sin. And do not spy or backbite one another.' (Surah 49:12)

Lying

'If you do not give up telling lies, God will have no need of you giving up food and drink (in fasting).' (Abu Dawud)

Pride

'Turn your face not away from people in scorn, and do not walk about in the earth exultantly; God loves not the proud and boastful. Be modest in your walk and lower your voice; the most hideous of voices to God is that of the ass!' (Surah 31:19)

Envy

'When you see another who is better off than you in respect of wealth, look on one who is below you. That is more proper, that you do not hold in contempt the favour of Allah towards you.' 'Beware of envy, for it eats up goodness as fire eats up fuel.'

Anger

'*Truly, anger spoils faith just as bitter aloes spoil honey.*' (*Ahmad*)

'*Allah holds back His punishment from him who holds back his anger.*' (*Baihaqi*)

Divisiveness

'*This is My straight path, so follow it, and do not follow other paths which will separate you from this path.*' (*Surah 6:153*)

Excess and extremism

'*O people of the Book! Do not exceed in your religion the bounds, trespassing beyond the truth.*' (*Surah 5:77*)

'*O believers, do not make unlawful those good things which Allah has made lawful for you, and commit no excess. God loves not those given to excess.*' (*Surah 5:87*)

These ethical values are shared with all serious followers of many religions – they are universal values. But in Islam, they are laid down as a duty.

Islamic ethics could be summarised by this one verse from the Qur'an and this one famous hadith:

'*Goodness and Evil cannot be equal. Repay evil with what is better, then he who was your enemy will become your intimate friend.*' (*Surah 41:34*)

'*You shall not enter Paradise until you have faith, and you cannot have faith until you love one another. Have compassion on those you can see, and He Whom you cannot see will have compassion on you.*' (*Muslim*)

24

—————— BIRTH ——————

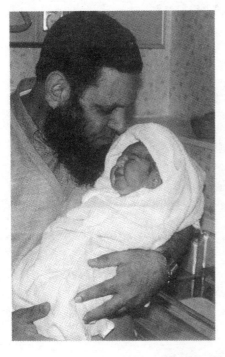

Muslims never regard babies as 'accidents' or 'mistakes' but as gifts from God. To be able to have children is a great blessing, one which many people do not appreciate.

A Muslim welcomes a new baby into the ummah as soon as it is born, by whispering the call to prayer (the adhan, beginning 'Allahu Akbar!') into the baby's right ear, and the command to rise and worship (the iqamah) in its left ear, sometimes using a hollow reed or tube. Thus the word 'God' is the first word the baby hears.

—————— Tahnik ——————

This little ceremony is the touching of the lips of the baby with honey or sweet juice or pressed dates, accompanied by prayers for the welfare of the child. This symbolises making the child 'sweet', obedient and kind.

Aqiqah

When the baby is seven days old, its head is shaved and the equivalent of the weight of the hair in gold or silver is given to the poor and needy, for invocation of blessings on the child. Even if the baby is bald, a donation is still given, which is usually well above the weight of the hair.

Sacrifice

The sacrifice of an animal is the ancient ritual of thanksgiving. Two animals are offered for a boy and one for a girl. The meat should be distributed among the poor and needy.

Naming

The choice of name is very important to a Muslim, and the Prophet even changed the names of some of his friends when he thought them unfortunate, ugly or insulting.

'Do not insult each other by nicknames.' (Surah 94:11)

Muhammad has now become the most common boy's name in the world, and the second most common is Ali (even before the Christian names Peter and John).

The Prophet's actual recommendation was: 'The most pleasing of names to Allah are Abdullah ('servant of Allah') and Abdur-Rahman ('servant of the Merciful One').

If a boy has the name Abdul, this means 'slave of', and should be followed by one of the ninety-nine names of God – for example, Abdul Karim ('slave of the Generous One'), or Abdul-Rahman (see above). Muslim babies are never named 'slave of' any human being, even Muhammad. Many Muslim girls take the names of women in the Prophet's family, such as Aisha, Fatima, Khadijah, Ruqaiyyah and Zainab.

The Prophet disapproved of names that suggested in a rather snobbish and conceited manner that the child had certain qualities or attributes (e.g. 'the sweet-tempered one', 'the beautiful one'), when this might not turn out to be the case at all.

Kunya names

Muslim parents of babies rather confusingly sometimes now drop their own names and take a *kunya* name; they call themselves 'father of' or 'mother of' the child – Abu Hussain, or Umm Hussain.

Circumcision – khitan

Circumcision, or *khitan*, is the cutting of the foreskin at the end of the penis, the practice of all those submitted to Allah, known through the revelations of the earliest prophets. This is usually done at the same time as the aqiqah, if the baby is well. If the child is weak or ill it can be delayed, but should be done as soon as possible.

In some countries the culture of the land leaves it until the boy is seven-to-ten-years-old, and it becomes a serious ordeal for the child. In Turkey, the young boys are dressed up like glittering princes, and are circumcised at a public party.

If circumcision is left until the boy is more than ten years old, this is considered shameful, and the parents are considered cruel and neglectful.

Bismillah

As soon as a child is able, he or she begins to learn the Qur'an. At the age of four or five a 'Bismillah' ceremony sometimes takes place in which a devout senior relative, or perhaps the Imam, invites the child to recite surat al-Fatihah and to write the alphabet in Arabic. The successful child feels very happy and proud. After this, the child learns how to perform wudu, and begins to have proper lessons in Islamic studies.

By the age of ten the child should know enough to perform the five daily prayers meaningfully on his or her own, should have started fasting, should be familiar with good Islamic manners and practices, and should have learned to be respectful, modest, clean and aware of haram and halal food.

25

MARRIAGE AND DIVORCE

'And among the signs of Allah is this, that He created for you mates, that you might live in tranquillity with them; and He has put love and mercy between your (hearts). Truly in that are signs (about the nature of Allah) for those who reflect.' (Surah 30:21)

As a good and devout home life is so essential to Islam, making a good marriage is of the utmost importance.

'Whoever has married has completed half of his faith.' (Baihaqi)

Marriage is not thought of in Islam as a mystical sacrament 'made in heaven' between two perfectly attuned souls, but as a social contract which brings rights and obligations to ordinary men and women, and which can only be successful when these are mutually respected and cherished.

It is not Islamic to think of marriages just in terms of a sex life, although this obviously has its important role; Muslims think of wives as potential mothers, and it is in the role of mother that a Muslim woman is most important.

'Do not marry for the sake of physical attraction; the beauty may be the cause of moral decline. Do not marry for the sake of wealth, for this may become the cause of disobedience. Marry rather on the grounds of religious devotion.' (Tirmidhi)

It is the mother who sees to the well-being of the family, and generally sets the standard for its morality, politeness, and the children's first learning about Islam. The father is the head of the family in Islam, but the mother is the heart of the family.

> *'The best of treasures is a good wife. She is pleasing to her husband's eyes, obedient to his word, and watchful over his possessions in his absence. And the best of you are those who treat your wives best.'*
> *(Abu Dawud, Ibn Majah)*

Bringing a new husband or wife into the family is therefore a very serious business and never to be taken lightly. It is intended to be a bonding for life.

Arranged marriages

Muslim marriages are frequently arranged by the parents of the young people, who seek to find good, compatible partners for their children. Young Muslims do not usually have the opportunities of western youngsters to meet and 'fall in love', and to be under the influence of love is considered to be a state of intoxication that can easily cloud the judgement.

It is not Islam for parents to force their youngsters into marriage with someone that son or daughter does not like. The normal procedure is to arrange a few meetings in a chaperoned situation (usually at other people's weddings or family gatherings), where they can meet and observe the prospective partner. If either side rejects the suggested partner, it can be done discreetly, without hurt feelings. Although the newspapers frequently report abuses, a forced marriage is actually invalid in Shariat law.

> *Aisha recorded that she asked the Prophet (pbuh) about the marriages of young girls whose guardians arranged matches for them. Was it necessary to consult the girl involved, or not. He said: 'Yes, she must be consulted.' (Muslim)*

Many Muslims marry their own relatives, and so their character and background will be well known. These days, Muslims are being alerted to the dangers of first cousin marriages, especially if this has been the practice for several (or many) generations, as it can increase the chances of inherited defects.

The dowry

Islam makes it obligatory for men to pay dowries to each of their wives, which remains the property of the wives. If, at a later stage, the marriage broke down, the wife could seek to divorce a husband unwilling to let her go, if she returned the dowry. If the husband divorced his wife, she would keep the dowry. Many women, therefore, are glad when a large dowry is negotiated, if they fear that their marriage might end in divorce.

In some cultures, the woman's family has to find the dowry, but this is not Islamic. The dowry system in Islam was not intended as a burden, but as a right to the wife.

The wedding

A truly Islamic wedding is a simple affair, and the bride does not even have to attend. If she chooses, she can send two witnesses of her agreement. The ceremony consists of readings from the Qur'an, and the exchange of vows in front of witnesses for both partners. No special religious official is necessary, but often the Imam is present.

In the United Kingdom, all marriages have to be registered at the registry office as well.

Many wedding customs, such as the bride's dress, are matters of culture. Many European brides these days wear a white wedding dress; Asian brides often wear a beautiful shalwar-qameez outfit (long shirt with baggy trousers beneath) in scarlet, embroidered with gold thread. The hands and feet are frequently patterned with henna.

Walima

This is the wedding party given for friends and family. It usually takes place either at the wedding or within three days of it. There is a sumptuous meal, and sometimes families go to enormous expense and invite hundreds of guests. The expense is in part defrayed by the system of the guests giving presents of money, the value of which is carefully recorded; presents of similar value are expected to be given when *their* relatives get married in turn.

However, it is important to realise that this is a cultural matter, and is not part of Islam. In fact, ostentation and expense is directly opposed to the spirit of Islam, and many families struggle to foot the enormous bill quite needlessly.

The main reason for the walima is to make public the fact that the bride and groom are now legally married and entitled to live together.

A newly married Muslim couple. The bride is wearing a traditional scarlet dress.

———— Mixed marriages ————

Muslim boys are permitted to marry Christian and Jewish girls, but not vice versa. This is because children usually take the religion of their fathers, and would, therefore, become non-Muslim. Muslims may only marry Hindus, Buddhists, etc. if the other party agrees to convert to Islam. This might sound harsh for societies used to young people meeting and falling in love at random, but in Islamic societies it would be extremely rare for a Muslim girl to request marriage to a non-Muslim boy.

This is a matter for concern to some Muslim parents who now live in non-Muslim societies, where their teenage daughters attend state schools and mingle freely with boys with whom they might fall in love. This is the main reason why Muslims seek single-sex schools for their children.

Any non-Muslim marrying a practising Muslim could find it very difficult and demanding to live with the Islamic regime.

—— Should husbands be obeyed? ——

The husband is always the head of the household in an Islamic marriage, but this does not mean that the woman is inferior in any way.

> *'A man is ruler of his family, and he will be questioned on the Day of Judgement about those under his care. A woman is ruler in the house of her husband, and she will be questioned about those under her care.' (Bukhari)*

A woman might be more intelligent, more educated, or more spiritually and morally gifted than her man. It is only to safeguard the smooth running of the home that a Muslim woman accepts a man as her leader. Therefore, a Muslim woman should take great care to marry a man whom she really does respect and who is worthy of her. Even so, she should only agree to obey him so long as what he requests does not break Islamic principles. Should he ask for something contrary to Islam, it is her duty *not* to obey him, but to obey Allah.

Polygamy

In any society where there is a greater number of women than men, strict monogamy means that many women will have no chance of marriage at all, and could more easily be tempted into immoral relationships.

In Islamic societies, where adultery is considered so serious that it can be punished by death, Muslim men are allowed to marry up to four wives, but only on certain conditions:

- the first wife has to give permission;
- later wives must not be a cause of distress to earlier ones;
- equal physical intimacy (or loving passion) is not something that is required (or possible), but the giving of equal time is;
- all wives must be treated fairly and equally as regards homes, food, clothing, gifts, and so on. Nights have to be spent with each in turn, unless a wife forgoes her turn.

A wife may have it written into her marriage contract that she should remain the only wife.

Two verses from the Qur'an have led many Muslims to argue that God really intended all marriages to be monogamous:

> *'Marry such women as may seem good to you, two, three or four. But if you fear that you will not be able to act justly, then marry one woman (only).' (Surah 4:3)*

> *'You will never be able to deal equitably with your wives, no matter how eager you may be to do so.' (Surah 4:129)*

However, it is a fact of history that the Prophet and all his Companions had more than one wife, and this would not have been possible had they thought it was counter to the will of Allah. (As we have seen, the Prophet remained monogamous throughout the twenty-four years of his marriage to Khadijah; after her death he married the widow, Sawdah, and was engaged to his friend's daughter, Aisha; and after the deaths of so many Muslims in battle the permission to marry up to four wives was given to Muslim men. The Prophet himself had special dispensation, and married thirteen women in total, all except Aisha being widows or divorcees needing care.)

Reasons for polygamy

The reason for polygamy in Islam is not, as some may think, because a man likes to have a large variety of women to choose from. That was the usual reason in the times before Islam gave women rights to put a stop to this practice.

Polygamy is considered a kindness when there is a large number of women without male protectors and companions, for example, after a war. Many women would rather share a husband than face many years of widowhood and loneliness, but it is a very generous, tolerant and understanding woman who would agree to share her husband.

However, the spirit of Islam is to defend the weak, and not to leave women to fend for themselves if they do not wish to do so. (Of course, if they choose not to marry, that is up to them.)

Polygamy is also allowed if a man's wife becomes so physically ill that she is no longer able to look after him or the family, or if she becomes mentally ill. Should a man be expected to live for the rest of his life without any sexual comfort, or should he divorce the unfortunate wife, or should he marry another?
If a man did fall in love with someone other than his wife, it is considered more honourable to marry the second woman rather than take her as a mistress, and to keep the first wife honourably rather than throw her out.

However, although as always one can easily find situations where abuses have taken place, true Islamic polygamy is always with the consent of the wife.

> *'The rights of a woman are sacred; ensure that women are maintained in the rights assigned to them.'*

———————————— Divorce ————————————

According to the Prophet, divorce was the thing permitted by Allah which He liked least.

> *'The most detestable act that God has allowed is divorce.' (Abu Dawud, Ibn Majah)*

Islam does not force couples to live together if the marriage has really broken down, although families and friends will do everything in their power to negotiate and heal the rift that has come between husband and wife. Divorce is considered as a very serious matter as it affects entire families.

(When one hears stories of people in the Middle East marrying and divorcing frequently and casually, this has nothing to do with Islam and is totally against the spirit of Islam.)

The actual procedure for divorce is reasonable, and is less of a strain than the western legal system. If the husband wishes to divorce his wife, he must announce this intention to her three times over a period of three months. If, at any time in this three months, the couple is reconciled and resumes a marital relationship, the divorce is cancelled. However, if, at the end of three months and after three announcements, marital relations have still not resumed, the divorce is considered valid. If the couple wishes to 'make it up' at a later stage, they have to be remarried.

If the couple goes through all this twice, and wish to remarry for a third time, in Islamic law they may not do this until the wife has legally married another man, and been divorced by him. Then she may remarry the first one if she wishes. (Fake marriages are not allowed in Shariat law.)

Wives may obtain a divorce from an Islamic court if the husband is sterile or impotent, if he refuses to maintain her; if he abuses or illtreats her; if he contracts some incurable repulsive disease, or becomes insane; if he deserts her or has gone away and not communicated with her for an unreasonable time; if he has been sent to prison for a very long period, or if it was discovered that he deceived her when they were drawing up their marriage contract or concealed important information concerning the marriage.

'Either keep your wife honestly, or put her away from you with kindness. Do not force a woman to stay with you who wishes to leave. The man who does that only injures himself.' (Surah 2:231)

Cultural differences (which are not Islam although they may be characteristic of various Muslim societies) are as strong for divorce as they are for marriage customs. Some societies make it almost impossible for a woman to survive after divorce; others make it very easy for a man to repudiate a wife unjustly. Neither of these things is Islamic.

When divorce is forbidden

For divorce to be valid in Islam, the husband must be sane, conscious and not under pressure from some outside party; he must not be under the influence of alcohol, drugs, or so angry that he did not fully appreciate what he was saying.

It is forbidden when the woman is menstruating, or is postnatal, when perhaps the husband's lack of sexual fulfilment might have made him tense, or led him to a hasty, ill-judged decision.

The waiting period under these circumstances, known as *iddah*, is usually three months, although it can be as long as nine months if the woman is pregnant. The wife is entitled to continue living at the house, even if she has been divorced, and is also entitled to full maintenance and to receive good treatment. She should not be forced out.

Custody of children

Normally, custody of children is given to the mother, but the responsibility of providing for them remains with the father.

> *'The mothers shall give suck to their offspring for two full years, if the father desires to complete the term. But he shall bear the cost of their food and clothing, on equitable terms. No soul shall have a burden laid on it greater than it can bear. No mother shall be treated unfairly on account of her child, nor father on account of his child . . . If they both decide to let the mother wean the child by mutual consent, there is no blame on them. If it is decided to have a foster-mother for the child, there is no blame provided the man pays the mother what was offered on equitable terms. Fear God, and know that God sees well all that you do.' (Surah 2:233)*

All settlements concerning children should be done amicably and without spite or rancour, and with the best interests of the children at heart. Sometimes, it was even considered best for the child to choose with which parent he or she would live:

> *'The Prophet said to a child: "This is your father and this is your mother, so take whichever of them you wish by the hand." He took his mother's hand, and she went away with him.' (Abu Dawud, Tirmidhi, Nisai, Ibn Majah and al-Hakim)*

In some circumstances, however, this is not considered wise. Muslim men who have married British women will often seek to keep custody of the children, for they would expect to remarry, or may take the children to their mother's household. This is considered better than the very common single parent situation in the United Kingdom, with women sometimes struggling to raise children in poor housing on very meagre finances.

26

THE TWILIGHT YEARS

'Your Lord orders that you . . . be kind to parents. If one or both of them attain old age with you, do not say one word of contempt to them, or repel them, but speak to them in terms of honour . . . and say, My Lord, bestow Your Mercy on them, as they cherished me when I was a child.' (Surah 17:23–24)

Many old people experience fear, helplessness and loneliness as they grow older and less capable of caring for themselves. As their friends and companions begin to die, and they become more frail and less able to get about, and their illnesses and wounds hang around longer, it is inevitable for them to turn their thoughts to 'When will it will be my turn?' and 'What will become of me?' Muslims regard duty to their parents as one of their prime duties.

Problems

As people become old, they often become confused, impatient, bad-tempered, or suffer the torment of continual aches and pains that give them no respite. They may also lack energy and become increasingly housebound, even chair or bed bound. Muslim families have a duty to be aware of the problems faced by old people, and not to turn their backs on them, or regard them as a nuisance. An increase of patience and kindness on the part of their family is what is required to cope with these problems.

Muslims do not regard it as acceptable to relegate the care of their old folk to strangers, unless there is absolutely no alternative. Just as the mother expects to care for and nurse her own child until it reaches independence, so the Muslim 'child' is expected to care of parents who are approaching the end of life, and to nurse them safely into the next life.

> 'May his nose be rubbed in dust who found his parents approaching old age and lost his right to enter Paradise because he did not look after them.' (Tirmidhi)

In fact, the Prophet thought care of parents so important that not even personal religious devotion should be used as an excuse for neglecting them.

> 'A person came seeking permission to participate in jihad, but the Prophet (pbuh) found out that he had parents living, and sent him away saying: "Go back to your parents and look after them."'
> (Muslim – and it is worth noting that these parents were not themselves Muslims at that time.)

Respect

One of the Prophet's most famous hadith concerned the respect a Muslim should show to his or her mother.

Abu Huraira recorded that a person asked Allah's Messenger (pbuh):

> 'Who of all people is the most deserving of the best treatment from my hand?' He said: 'Your mother.' The man said again: 'Then, who is next?' He said: 'Again, it is your mother.' He said: 'Then who?' He said: 'Again, it is your mother.' He said: 'Then who?' Thereupon, he said: 'Then it is your father.' (Muslim)

It is a disgraceful thing to see children ordering their parents about and being rude to them, or treating them as if they were imbeciles. Muslims see their old folk as wise guides, with a lifetime of experience behind them. No Muslim should ever regard it as being beneath his or her dignity to be kind to old folk.

'He who has no compassion for our little ones, and does not acknowledge the honour due to our elders, is not one of us.' (Tirmidhi)

——— Some practical details ———

Muslims consider it impolite for a young person to call an adult by his or her first name, or to do in front of them anything of which they might disapprove, such as smoking.

Young people should not walk in front of old people, or sit down before they do. They should not interrupt them, or hurry them in their speech, or argue with them – even if they do not agree.

They should help them without being asked, and avoid doing anything that irritates them.

They should never draw attention to the care and support they are giving them, or point out what they are spending on them, to make them feel a burden, or feel guilty.

Parents are usually much more sensitive to any act of discourtesy towards them from their own children than from any other people. Muslims strive to see to it that they should never suffer from hurtful behaviour or speech.

'Allah defers the punishment of all your sins until the Day of Judgement except one – disobedience to parents. For that, Allah punishes the sinner in this life, before death.' (Baihaqi)

27

– DEATH AND BURIAL –

For a devout Muslim, death is not something to be feared, although it obviously makes people sad. Muslims know that the time of their death will not be of their choosing, but when God wishes to call their souls back to Him. Life is God's gift, and the length of one's life is His grant. The true Muslim accepts this as part of the submission to Allah, and greets the possibility of death with the phrase *'Amr Allah'* – 'At Your Command, O Lord.'

Other people, of course, are very distressed by their lives and pray earnestly to have them ended, but God knows best and people who are required to live on, despite their hurts and pains, must be patient and try to find the faith to make the best of their circumstances, and not concentrate on the worst side of it.

At the deathbed

Muslims hope to die surrounded by their loved ones, family and friends. However, even if they have to die alone, they should not feel alone, for they know the angels will help them.

For those tending the dying, a tactful, respectful and sympathetic atmosphere is recommended as the best way; not becoming so 'holy' that the dying person is irritated, or feels they are being 'hurried' out of this life, and not being so casual that the dying one feels they are not important, or not loved.

If possible, the bed should be turned so that they can be facing Makkah, with feet in the direction of the Ka'aba. Prayers should not be intrusive, but as the dying one finds comfortable. Many relatives will pray using words from Surah Ya-Sin (Surah 36 – 'Surely We will give life to the dead', etc), though the reciter must pray inaudibly so as not to disturb the dying person. It is always considered the best thing if a believer dies with prayer, or thoughts of Allah.

'If anyone's last words are "There is no God but Allah", he will enter Paradise.' (Abu Dawud)

This is not a matter of fanaticism, however, and God is not disappointed if these are not their last words; He knows best. What is important is that one dies in the state of belief.

The Prophet's sunnah was to settle everything before he died, so that his mind was at rest. Any debts should be paid (or settled by relatives as soon as possible after the death of the loved one), and forgiveness requested for any sins committed against anyone, either sins committed, or sins of omission. Then, the dying one may feel at peace, and may relax and prepare for the next stage of life.

——————— Duties after death ———————

When the loved one has died, the eyes should be gently closed, and a prayer said, such as the Prophet's own prayer (over his friend Abu Salama) –

O Allah, forgive Your servant, raise him to high rank among those who are rightly guided; make him as a guardian of his descendants who survive him. Forgive us and him, O Lord of the Universe; make his grave spacious and grant him light in it.' (Muslim)

The deceased should be given the final ritual wash. Although Muslims believe that the soul departed at the moment of death, and what is left behind is nothing but an empty shell, nevertheless the mortal remains of a Muslim should be treated with dignity, love and respect, and the last services done to them in a prayerful and loving atmosphere.

Muslims therefore believe the final washing should not be done by strangers, but by members of the family, preferably male relatives for men, and female relatives for women. A husband is allowed to perform this duty for his wife, and a wife for her husband. The Prophet said to his wife Aisha:

'If you should die before me, I shall wash you, shroud you, offer prayer over you and bury you.' (Ibn Majah)

(The School of Abu Hanifa does not allow a man to wash his wife, but this does not appear to be sunnah. Ali washed his wife, the Prophet's daughter Fatima, with his own hands.)

If there is no relative available, the duty falls on any member of the community, to see it is done as decently as possible.

If males are washing females, or vice versa, their hands should be covered so that they do not touch the naked bodies.

If clean water cannot be found (as in some circumstances), tayammum may be done with sand if available. Muslims are not obliged to wash unbelievers, aborted foetuses, dead bodies that have been bomb-blasted; any martyrs are traditionally buried 'with their blood'. In these cases, they are usually shrouded in their clothes.

If pilgrims die in ihram, they should be buried as pilgrims, with heads uncovered (for men) and faces unveiled (for women).

For these reasons, Muslims always appreciate hospitals that are aware of their beliefs and customs, and allow the relatives to take their dead away, or to do the washing and shrouding themselves.

Shrouding

It is not commendable to use expensive materials, but three white winding sheets for a man, and five for a woman. The shrouding could, however, be two sheets, or even one, provided it covers the whole of the body.

The sheets are spread out, one on top of the other, with the final one being the longest and widest. The deceased is lifted and laid on top of them and perfumed with incense. Then the edge of the top winding sheet is folded over the deceased's right side, and the other edge over the left side. The second and third sheets are treated in the same way. These are all fastened in place round the deceased and only unfastened when he or she is laid in the grave.

If no sheet can be found big enough to cover the entire body, then the head should be covered with it, and grass or paper placed over the legs. If the dead are many, two or three may be shrouded together and buried in one grave.

A woman's shrouding consists of a loin-cloth to bind her upper legs, waist wrapper to tie it in place, a shift, a head veil (after her hair is plaited, if it is long) and the final winding sheet.

— Funeral Prayer – Salat ul-Janaza —

This is a collective obligation and has to be performed by at least one Muslim. The best person to perform it is whoever the deceased chose personally, providing that person is not immoral or an unbeliever. After that, preference goes to the Imam or his deputy, the deceased's father, or grandfather, then son, grandson, or closest male relative.

The whole prayer is made standing; there is no prostration as in the normal prayer.

One of the Prophet's famous prayers was:

> *'O Allah, forgive him, have mercy on him, give him peace and absolve him. Receive him with honour, and make his grave spacious; wash him with water, snow and hail. Cleanse him from faults as You would cleanse a white garment from impurity. Give him an abode more excellent than his abode was here, with a family better than his family, and a companion better than his companion. Admit him to the garden and protect him from the torment of the grave and the torment of the fire.' (Muslim)*

— The funeral —

Cremation is not allowed in Islam.

People should always stand in respect when a funeral passes. The Prophet recommended that it was more respectful to walk than to ride. (Hiring funeral cars is almost universal in the West. The principle is to be respectful without being ostentatious. If there are walkers, they should precede the vehicle.) He allowed women to accompany processions, but did not recommend it.

The grave

Again, this should be simple and not ostentatious. Extravagance is forbidden in Islam, and there is no class system for the dead. At the graveside, people should remain standing until the person has been buried (although they may sit to wait if they have arrived before the cortege).

The grave should reach the depth of a man's chest, and preferably have a qiblah niche in it. It is preferable if the cemetery is a Muslim one, or at least a part of it made over to Muslims, so that the graves may be orientated towards Makkah.

A woman's body should be lowered in by men within her family, and all bodies are placed in the grave legs first. The deceased are placed on their right sides, with their faces in the direction of the Ka'aba, and supported so that they do not roll over on to their backs. The fastening of the shroud is undone, and bricks, canes, or leaves set in place so that no earth falls on the body.

A little earth is then sprinkled into the grave, saying:

'We created you from it, and return you into it, and from it We will raise you a second time.' (Surah 20:55)

Then the earth is heaped over, while the people pray. The surface of the grave should be raised a hand's-breadth so that it will be recognised as a grave and not trodden on. It is also considered very disrespectful to sit on graves, or lean against them.

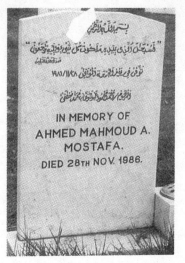

The grave may be marked with a headstone, but Muslims should not spend money on tombstones or memorials. Instead, donations may be given to the poor. Making structures over the grave or plastering them is considered a pre-Islamic practice, and is, therefore, forbidden.

A simple, Muslim head-stone.

—— Making graves into shrines ——

It was, and is, the culture of many places to go to the graves of saintly persons for superstitious motives, to pray to the holy soul to help them or grant them offspring, and so on. This is actually forbidden in Islam.

Prayers may be said at the graveside for the deceased, but not *to* them, which is a form of shirk.

Mosques should not be erected over graves, and Muslim purists feel that the Prophet would disapprove strongly of places where this has been done. He was buried in Aisha's room, but this has now been incorporated into the Mosque at Madinah, and again, some purists feel this is wrong.

—————— Condolences ——————

Muslims are expected to mourn a husband or wife for four months and ten days. For other deceased, the period is three days and nights. Although one is naturally very sad at a death, the Muslim faith is that people will go to their reward, and the only ones really to be mourned are those who rejected belief in God and lived in such a way that would earn punishment.

The custom of holding *rawdahs* or commemoration services on the third day, or the fortieth day, or the anniversary of someone's death, have no basis in Qur'an or sunnah, but are matters of tradition.

28

—— ISLAMIC DRESS ——

People who have travelled about the world will be very aware that there are all sorts of styles and garments that qualify as Islamic dress.

Basically, the principles are modesty and cleanliness. What people actually wear is very much governed by the society in which they live, but Islamic garments are always modest and, if possible, clean.

Some Western women may regard Muslim women's dress as dull, and some kind of restriction – but this is not how Muslim women see it. They prefer to dress modestly, and regard revealing and sexually provocative clothing as pandering to the lowest instinct of the male, and encouraging men to look on women as 'sex objects' rather than equal and independent characters. They wish men to notice their minds and characters, and not their physical bodies.

'Every religion has a characteristic, and the characteristic of Islam is modesty.' (Ibn Majah)

Muslim women may wear any type of clothing provided it is not attention-seeing by being either too revealing, transparent, too brash, too tight or too short, and so on. Some clothes are regarded as presenting women as 'naked even though they are clothed', and their only object must be to stir the passions of men and tempt them, which is neither fair, nor kind, nor sensible.

There are few particular rules for men's wear, except for pilgrims in *ihram*, and when it comes to the time of prayer. At prayer times, even in the most primitive conditions, men must be covered at least from navel to knee.

Men are not allowed to wear garments made of silk, unless they have a skin disorder that requires it. They should not wear jewellery other than a wedding ring, which should be made of silver and not gold.

——————— Female modesty ———————

Women are allowed to wear gold and other jewellery. Transparent blouses or sleeves are not approved of, and it is worth noting that many western blouses, even those with long sleeves, are thin enough to reveal the underwear beneath. This is not approved of in Islam.

Many forms of trousers are acceptable for women, Asian women in particular favouring the shalwar-qameez outfits of a long shirt, with baggy trousers beneath. These can be as colourful or decorative as individuals desire, but they should be modest. Tight trousers are not approved of in Islam, however, many Muslim women wear western-style trousers, with an over-shirt or blouse long enough to be acceptable.

Malaysian girls, modestly dressed.

Hijab

Hijab (or veiling) indicates modesty in dress and behaviour. Muslim women do not wish to display their physical beauty in public. That is something reserved for their husbands, for whom they should make themselves as beautiful and attractive as possible.

> *'Believing women should lower their gaze and guard their modesty; they should not display their ornaments except as is normal, they should draw their veils over their bosoms and not display their beauty except to their close male relatives.' (Surah 24:30–31; the surah gives the precise list of these relatives)*

The one item of clothing that marks out most Muslim women is the hijab veil, a headscarf of any material and in any style that hides the hair from public view. This was the sunnah of the Prophet's wives, and the Prophet himself said on one occasion that nothing of a female past the age of puberty should be seen except her face and hands.

The fact that millions of Muslim women do not wear hijab any longer does not alter the fact that it is sunnah. Some Muslim women have resisted the traditional hijab of their cultural communities because it is so hot, cumbersome, and the pugnacious attitude of males to their women who don't wear it has put them in revolt.

However, most Muslim women regard the wearing of some sort of hijab as part of their discipline, and where there is a resurgence of Islamic faith, women are beginning to take the hijab again in increasing numbers.

Islam did not require women to wear the black veils frequently seen in Islamic societies, nor did it require them to hide their faces. These things are a matter of culture, although nowadays only Muslim women do them. The all-covering sheet (also called a *chador* or *burqa*) actually originated in high caste Hindu and Persian Christian society as a form of social snobbery.

Nowadays, women in Iran and Saudi Arabia can be arrested and abused if they do not wear them. However, there is no stipulation in Qur'an or hadith that these garments are in any way compulsory, and any male trying to force a woman in matters of religion is breaking the Islamic injunction against coercion in religion, and going completely and ironically against the true spirit of Islam.

It is particularly important to emphasise these things in societies where 'fundamentalists' have gained the upper hand over moderate Muslims, because there is a danger in those circumstances of Muslim extremist men becoming so obsessive and overzealous on women's clothing that it leads to repression and even cruelty, all in total opposition to the spirit of the Islam they claim to be serving.

29

—— ISLAMIC DIET ——

In Islam, foods are either halal or haram. That which is halal is allowed, and that which is haram is forbidden. This is not a matter of likes and dislikes, but of discipline and submission. As in every other walk of life, Allah gave instructions for the guidance of believers, and even the basic need to eat is under discipline.

Allah created all the goodness of the earth and its produce for humanity to utilise, but requested certain restrictions.

> 'O believers! Eat of the good things that We have provided for you, and be grateful to God if it is Him you worship. He has only forbidden you meat of an animal that dies of itself, and blood, and the flesh of pigs, and that on which any other name has been invoked besides that of God.' (Surah 2:172)

> 'The strangled, the beast beaten down, the beast that died by falling, the beast gored, and that devoured by beasts of prey . . . and anything sacrificed to idols.' (Surah 5:4)

———————————— Pork ————————————

First, no Muslim should ever eat the flesh of the pig, or any pork product. This does not mean a Muslim convert simply giving up sausages, bacon, ham and pork pies. It also means checking whether or not a product includes animal fat, for that fat might well have come from a pig.

In the East, the pig is regarded as a very unclean animal, with good reason, for it eats excrement. In some places it is deliberately used to gobble up excrement. Therefore, no Muslim would contemplate eating it, for it is simply regarded as disgusting. To put a piece of pork on a Muslim's plate would have the same effect as putting excrement on their plate; some Muslims would be physically sick.

Many Muslims are quite frightened when they come to the United Kingdom, because they know that the populace is fed on pork. They believe it is the cause of all sorts of ailments and allergies, and there is increasing medical evidence that this may very well be so. In the East, pork meat is certainly riddled with minute worms and causes all sorts of horrible disorders.

Other meats

Other meats, such as chicken, beef, lamb, and goat, are allowed for Muslims, provided they have been slaughtered by the halal method, which is to cut the jugular vein with a very sharp knife, accompanied by prayer. Pronouncing the name of God is a rite to call attention to the fact that they are not taking life thoughtlessly, but with the permission of God for food.

Muslims believe that to cut the throat is not only the kindest method of killing an animal, but also that it is beneficial for the person who will eat the meat. They claim that the blood congeals in animals that are stunned, electrocuted, shot or clubbed, whereas to cut the jugular vein allows the beast to lose consciousness immediately and the blood to rush out freely. Muslims leave the animal's carcase to bleed completely.

Muslims are not allowed to eat the meat of any creature which has died of itself, or been strangled, or clubbed to death, or savaged or gored by other animals. By analogy, birds of prey, animals with claws and fangs, rodents, reptiles and insects, with the exception of locusts, are also haram.

Halal shops

For this reason, Muslims in the United Kingdom usually buy all their meat from halal butchers, or special Muslim shops, not regarding the meat in ordinary butchers' shops to be acceptable. In Muslim countries all meat would be slaughtered by the halal method, so there would not be any problem of finding a supplier.

As the Jews follow the same rules of slaughter for their kosher meat, Muslims are allowed to eat meat from Jewish shops, if they wish.

Some Muslims take the point of view that since the last revealed verse of the Qur'an says that both Jewish and Christian food was lawful for Muslims, then Muslims who live in Christian countries should be allowed to eat commercial meat (apart from pork), so long as they pronounce the name of God on it at the time of eating. (Surrah 516)

However, many Muslims would rather do without meat than do this; nowadays halal shops are becoming more common, so the problems are lessened.

Other foods

All fish, fruits and vegetables are halal, and all grain and root crops. However, Muslims should still check all packets for ingredients, for many biscuits, cakes, ice-creams and soups contain the fat of animals or animal gelatine. Unless it is kosher, or of vegetable origin, gelatine is usually made from animal hide trimmings, including those of the pig; it is found in many desserts, creams, cake fillings, sweets, commercial yoghurts, and other foods.

Waste

Muslims believe that food should never be wasted. If anything is left over, it should be given away to the needy, or fed to the birds or the animals that come into the garden.

—— When no halal food is available ——

In cases of absolute necessity, Muslims may eat what there is available.

> '*If one is forced because there is no other choice, neither craving nor transgressing, there is no sin in him. Indeed, Allah is forgiving, merciful.' (Surah 2:173 – see also 5:4)*

No Muslim should eat the haram food eagerly, or become accustomed to it, or use this principle as an excuse to enjoy it under the pretext of necessity.

30

SPECIFIC PROBLEMS FOR MUSLIMS —— LIVING IN THE —— UNITED KINGDOM

Islam is the fastest-growing religion in the United Kingdom at the present time, and the number of Muslims has now reached the two million mark. This is partly because Muslims tend to have quite large families, and is also due to an increasing number of converts.

Balancing the number of Muslims born into already-Muslim families are the rather large numbers of men and women who find the Islamic life too much for them, and in the freedom of western society, choose to abandon it. These tend to fall into two categories; youngsters who have succumbed to the allure of the western social scene with its alcohol, pubs, nightclubs, discos and so on, and women who have rebelled against the over strict rules (which are not in themselves necessarily Islamic) that their parents have tried to maintain over them, including arranged marriages. It is too early to guess how many of these will come back to their roots later, in the same way that people leave the Christian church and come back to it in later life.

Segregation

First comes the question of the segregation of the sexes at puberty. Muslims prefer their girls to be taught in an all-female environment, and vice versa, and even when they are sent to single sex schools, if these are available, there is still the question of the sex of the teacher. Muslims would prefer the same system that can be found in Muslim societies; female teachers for girls, and male teachers for boys. They would also prefer at least some of the teachers on the staff to be Muslim by faith as well.

For these reasons, many Muslims are now attempting to set up their own schools. However, more girls need to be encouraged to take up further education if there is to be a supply of female Muslim teachers.

Dress

Second, Muslims prefer their girls to cover their legs and wear hijab if possible. Some schools do not allow this, but generally the situation has eased with more understanding in recent years, and most schools will allow Muslim girls to wear trousers as part of their school uniform. Schools need to realise that 'Muslim' does not equal 'Asian', and should make the same allowances for white Muslim girls.

Mixed sports lessons, especially swimming, are not approved of, and Muslim girls are not encouraged to wear the same revealing swimsuits that are common in the United Kingdom. They certainly should not wish to wear bikinis. For most sports, a track suit is approved, or some modest covering such as a bodysuit with shorts worn over it.

Sex education

Muslims are very wary of their young being taught sexual matters by people whose own morals they are not sure of. It is all too easy these days for teachers to be living together while unmarried, or assuming that young people are all enjoying 'relationships', and so forth.

Muslims are also wary of sex education being carried out when pupils are too young, or where boys and girls are being taught together. They feel this is something better left to the parents.

However, Muslims are not against sex education as such, so long as it is taught in a Muslim moral context.

Religious Education

Since Religious Education is still compulsory in State schools, this can be another problem area, for several reasons. First, if the school presents a wholly Christian syllabus, the Muslim child may suffer from the notion that Islam is 'wrong'. Second, even where a multi-faith syllabus is taught, there is still the danger of faiths other than Christianity being 'talked down'.

Another problem is that, with the best will in the world, different faiths are sometimes taught by people who know hardly anything about them, and in fact, teach them wrongly. This used to be very common, but with today's highly researched textbooks it is not so great a problem as it used to be.

When it comes to celebrating holy days, Muslims sometimes feel very awkward because of the emphasis placed on Christmas and Easter. Although Muslims believe in the Virgin Birth of Jesus, they do not believe that this made him 'Son of God', or that he was 'born to save us from our sins', except in the sense that he was a Messenger of God teaching people the way to salvation.

Other subjects on the syllabus

Other subjects on the syllabus that cause problems for a Muslim are English lessons, when the books studied present immorality; music lessons, when pop music with sexual lyrics or sexually provocative rhythms are played; and history lessons, which sometimes present a very biased and colonialist point of view of the world's history – usually referring to the peak period of Islamic culture in Europe as being the Dark Ages.

—————— Muslim Education ——————

Many immigrants have not really taken on board the necessity of giving their young people a genuine education in Islam. It is not enough to hope they will just pick it up as they go along simply because they were born into Muslim families; it needs to be taught, and taught properly.

In Muslim countries governments provide education consistent with the Islamic heritage and religious beliefs, but Muslims cannot reasonably expect more than tolerance on the part of United Kingdom authorities.

Most mosques try to impart some Islamic knowledge to their young by having lessons at the mosque after school or at the weekend. This has potential, but is frequently not really satisfactory. It is now widely acknowledged that it taxes, bores and stresses children without providing any significant degree of knowledge or understanding of the faith.

'The first generation Muslim immigrants have displayed an impressive commitment to what they have interpreted to be their faith and tradition, but there have been disadvantages too. Since these Muslims could not always clearly distinguish between Islam as a universal faith on the one hand, and the narrow cultural interpretations of Islam prevalent on the Indian sub-continent, some of the materials and attitudes found in mosque schools are sometimes irrelevant to true Islam, and often, inadvertently, opposed to it. Most supplementary schools have poor facilities . . . Children remain on the wrong wavelength mentally because of the speed with which they transfer from the State school to the mosque school. The ethos of the two types could hardly be more different. The result is a tired, unmotivated pupil who sees evening classes at the mosque as simply a burden he must shoulder for fear of his parents' (*The Muslim Parents' Handbook*, Shabbir Akhtar, Ta-Ha Publishers Ltd, 1993, p.69).

Many Muslims now realise that they must establish Muslim schools in the United Kingdom, but it is an uphill struggle; there is no tradition of them, and there is active resistance to them as it is feared they will become breeding-grounds for militancy and extremism.

—————— Friday prayers ——————

Many Muslim males would like to attend the compulsory Friday prayers at the mosque, but are not able to leave the school or the workplace. Some employers are more sympathetic than others about the two hours or so an employee would be missing from work. At school, it is sometimes possible for Muslim youngsters to gather together to pray, but there are not always facilities for this, or for the washing that comes before prayer.

Medical treatment

Muslims prefer women to be treated by women, and men by men, and this is not always possible in hospital/medical conditions. However, it is usually possible to choose one's General Practitioner (GP). Hospitals are not always very sympathetic to mass visiting from large families; there is sometimes a language problem, with very frightened patients unable to understand what is going on, although nowadays people can often be found who can speak an Asian language.

When a Muslim dies in hospital, the family is grateful for sympathetic authorities that allow relatives to take the dead away quickly for washing and burial.

Dogs

Muslims are not against dogs as such, but if their saliva touches the clothing, it is rendered unclean for prayer, and the Muslim would have to go home and change.

Planes going to the Middle East often use sniffer dogs to find hidden drugs and explosives. This annoys many Muslims who like their aircraft to be ritually clean so that they can pray in them when it comes to the appropriate times.

Racism and intolerance

Sadly, this can always be found in any country. Muslims have to be tolerant themselves, and understand that if some individuals make life unpleasant for them, there are countless others who are ashamed of the racism and intolerance that ignorant people sometimes show.

Muslim organisations

There are hundreds of Muslim organisations, including the World Muslim League, UK Council of Imams, World Sufi Council, Islamic Council of Europe, World Islamic Mission, UK Islamic Mission, the Muslim Institute, the Islamic Cultural Centre, the Muslim League, and so on. In fact, it is said that the number of Islamic organisations actually exceeds the number of mosques in the United Kingdom.

It is now increasingly being realised that there is a danger in many of these organisations. Many of them are creations of particular individuals with rather inflated egos, and have committees which are only there to rubber-stamp the policies of the founders; and anyone who flatters the founder is promoted, all in the name of Islam.

There is a horrifying un-Islamic upsurge of hypocrisy, deceit, dishonesty and backbiting in many Muslim attempts at organisation or communal activity. Frequently certain prominent members tend to force individuals to conform to their particular interpretations of Islam. This leads to lack of tolerance, lack of humility, lack of real choice, the exploitation of the many by the few, and the danger of Muslims adopting a kind of 'Muslim of the Year' award mentality.

In terms of the effectiveness of these organisations towards British society, the results are appalling – most of them being so engrossed with their own quarrels with each other that they cannot concentrate on the real important issues facing the community. When British society observes these unedifying rivalries, it simply fuels their contempt (or even hatred) for Islam.

UK converts

Surprisingly, perhaps, Islam is growing very fast among United Kingdom converts – not through the off-putting activities of the Islamic missionaries, but being drawn by observing the polite, decent and hospitable way of life of ordinary Muslim people. Some have become fascinated with Islam through what they have observed while on holidays abroad. Others, particularly the intellectuals, have appreciated the spiritual richness of Sufism. Most converts are self-taught, and have come into Islam through their ability to read widely, and study on their own.

God moves in mysterious ways. It is not unknown for British women to be attracted to Islam by a somewhat villainous Muslim male, only to be put off and sent packing again by the extremely devout sectarians at the mosque.

However, the small United Kingdom community is characterised by enormous energy and enthusiasm. Some leaders now attract quite wide audiences, and their influence will inevitably increase as they have thought the issues through carefully, and are increasingly not afraid to speak out.

It may well be the task of Muslim converts to interpret Islam's spiritual message to the western world, and even to help wavering ethnic Muslims, who are succumbing to the secular society.

Muslims of many races meet together at the mosque.

GLOSSARY

adhan – call to prayer
akhira – life after death
al-Ghaib – the unseen universe
al-hujr al-aswad – the black stone
al-kiswah – the black cloth on Ka'aba
al-Qadr – predestination
amal – action
ansars – the Helpers of Madinah
aqiqah – cut hair of new baby
ashurah – 10th Muharram (death of Husain)
asr – the mid-afternoon prayer
ayah – Qur'an verse
ayatollah – leading shi'ite imam
burqa – fully covering garment
chador – covering sheet
du'a – personal prayer
eid al-adha – feast of sacrifice
eid ul-fitr – feast to end Ramadan
fajr – the pre-sunrise prayer
fard – obligatory
fiqh – study of Islamic law
ghusl – complete bath
hadith – sayings of the Prophet
hafiz(pl. huffaz) – knows the Qur'an by heart
hajj – pilgrimage
halal – permitted
haram – forbidden
hijab – the veil
ibadah – worship

ihram – pilgrim garments
ihsan – realisation
ijma – consensus of legal opinion
ijtihad – working out Islamic principles
imam – leader of congregation
iman – faith
iqamah – second call to prayer
isha – the night prayer
jahannam – hell
jama'ah – congregation
jamra – pillar representing devil
jannam – heaven, Paradise
jihad – striving for God
jinn – lesser spirit beings
ka'aba – Makkah cube-shaped shrine
khalifa – (Caliph) successor
khamr – intoxicant
khitan – circumcision
khutbah – sermon
kunya – parent's name taken from child
lailat ul-bara'at – Night of Blessing (full moon before Ramadan)
lailat ul-isra wal miraj – Night of Prophet's ascent to heaven
lailat ul-Qadr – the Night of Power (descent of the Qur'an)
madhdhab – school of Islamic law
maghrib – the nightfall prayer
masjid – mosque
medrassah – mosque school
mihrab – niche showing direction of Makkah
mimbar – pulpil for sermon
minaret – tower for call to prayer
muezzin – (muadhdhin) – person who calls to prayer
mubah – action left to conscience
muhajirun – the Emigrants from Makkah
mujtahid – religious scholar
muta – temporary marriage
nafs – soul
niyyah – intention
polygamy – multiple marriage
purdah – seclusion of women
qisas – 'eye for eye' revenge
Qur'an – Holy Book
rakah – unit of prayer movements

ramadan – fasting month
rawdah – gathering to commemorate the dead
riba – interest on loaned money
risalah – prophecy
salah – ritual prayer
salat ul-janaza – funeral prayer
sawm – fasting
shahadah – statement of belief, bearing witness
shariah – the Way of Islam
shi'ite – party of Ali sectarian
shirk – the division of the unity of God
subhah – prayer beads
sufi – religious mystic
suhur – dawn meal before fasting
sujud – prostration in prayer
sunnah – the Prophet's example
sunni – mainstream Muslim
surah – Qur'an chapter
taharah – purity
talaq – divorce
tajwid – art of correct pronunciation
tarawih – Ramadan prayers
tariqa – Sufi 'way' or 'order'
tasawwuf – spiritual insight in Islam
tasbih – prayer beads
taqwa – God-consciousness
tawhid – the One-ness of God
tayammum – 'dry' ritual wash
tilawah – reading with intent
ulema – religious teachers
ummah – the 'family' of Islam
umrah – pilgrimage not at Hajj time
walima – wedding party
wudu (wuzu) – ritual wash
wuquf – the 'stand' at Arafat
zakah – religious tax
zawiya – Sufi training centre
zina – adultery
zuhur – the mid-day prayer

RECOMMENDED BOOK LIST ——

Islam between East and West – Aliya Izetbegovic, American Trust Publications, 1984
Islam, the Way of Submission – Solomon Nigosian, Crucible, 1987
Islam – Rosalyn Kendrick, Heinemann, 1989
What is Islam? – C. Horrie, Star, 1990.
Thinking about God – Ruqaiyyah Waris Maqsood, American Trust Publications, 1994
Islam, its meaning and message – ed Khurshid Ahmad, Islamic Foundation, 1976.
What Everyone should know about Islam and Muslims – S. Haneef, Kazi Publications, 1985
The Elements of Islam – Shaykh Fadhlalla Haeri, Elements, 1993
The Elements of Sufism – Shaykh Fadhlalla Haeri, Element, 1990
The Qur'an – Ruqaiyyah Waris Maqsood, Heinemann, 1993
The Lawful and the Prohibited in Islam – Yusuf al-Qaradawi, Shorouk International, 1985
Hadith Literature, its origin, development and special features – Muhammad Zubayr Siddiqui, Islamic Texts Society, 1993
Morals and Manners in Islam – Marwan Ibrahim al-Kaysi, Islamic Foundation, 1986
The Way of Islam – Ruqaiyyah Waris Maqsood, Ta-Ha, 1994
For Heaven's Sake – Ruqaiyyah Waris Maqsood, Ta-Ha, 1994
Islamic Awakening between Rejection and Extremism – Yusuf al-Qaradawi, International Institute of Islamic Thought, 1991
Women and Gender in Islam – Leila Ahmed, Yale University, 1992
The Muslim Woman's Handbook – Huda Khattab, Ta-Ha, 1993
The Assassins – E. Burman, Crucible, 1987

INDEX